THE HELPFUL GUIDE TO

DAYS OUT

WITH KIDS

1999/2000

WEST COUNTRY
EDITION

CW00797960

"DEDICATED WITH LOVE AND A
BIG THANK YOU TO JACOB FOR
CHECKING OUT ALL THE GIFT
SHOPS, TO THEA FOR SLEEPING A
LOT – AND TO CHRISTPHER FOR
EVERYTHING HE DID TO HELP ME
REACH THE FINISHING LINE"

WITH THANKS TO: NICK
PRATT, SAMANTHA AND EDWARD;
POLLY PRING AND HER FAMILY
WHO TOOK ON A CHUNK OF THE
RESEARCH AND REPORTING;
PARTICULAR THANKS TO BIG SISTER
CAROLINE CLEMENTS AND PARTNER
JON PRING FOR INVALUABLE
SUPPORT, ENCOURAGEMENT AND
TYPING.

THE HEINZ GUIDE TO DAYS OUT

WITH KIDS

1999/2000 *EDITION*

TRIED-AND-TESTED FUN FAMILY OUTINGS IN THE WEST COUNTRY

PHILIPPA MAY
ROXANE PRATT

BON•BON
PUBLISHING

FIRST PUBLISHED IN 1999 BY
BON•BON PUBLISHING
24 ENDLESHAM ROAD
LONDON SW12 8JU

ISBN   1-901411-28-1

SERIES EDITOR JANET BONTHRON
DESIGN BY CAROLINE GRIMSHAW
ILLUSTRATIONS BY SAM TOFT

PRINTED & BOUND IN FINLAND BY
WERNER SÖDERSTRÖM OSAKEYHTIÖ

Dear Reader

This is the fourth edition of the Heinz Guide to Days Out with Kids, which continues to be a family favourite.

This really is now the definitive guide of its type and we are proud to be associated with it. We like to think that Heinz foods play a small part in virtually every family's life, so it's very appropriate that we should be sponsoring a book which can help parents make the most of their time with their families.

I hope you find this new edition a useful source of reference and inspiration.

ERIC SALAMON
HJ HEINZ

More about Heinz

Henry John Heinz was little more than a kid himself when he established his food business. At the age of 16 he began to bottle dried and grated horseradish from the family garden of his home in Sharpsburg, Pennsylvania.

He packed his product in clear glass bottles so that his customers could see he was selling only horseradish - without bits of turnip or other cheap fillers that other people used. Although he could not have known it at the time, he was starting a venture which was to grow into one of the world's great food enterprises.

In 1886 the British got to sample Heinz products for the first time. Henry Heinz visited London with five cases of products and called on Fortnum and Mason, who promptly bought the lot. The first British factory was established in 1905 in Peckham and a custom-made factory was built at Harlesden in north London in the mid 1920s.

That factory still stands and is an important production centre, but it is dwarfed by the factory built in Kitt Green

near Wigan in 1959, Europe's largest food factory. Today there are 360 Heinz products in the UK alone, ranging from well-known favourites like Heinz Baked Beans and Heinz Spaghetti through to all sorts of fun meal time treats like Thomas the Tank Engine pasta shapes, Heinz Baked Beans with Pork Sausages and Heinz Spaghetti Hoops with Hot Dogs.

HENRY J HEINZ

A history of Heinz

1844	Henry John Heinz born, Sharpsburg, Pennsylvania
1869	HJ Heinz Company formed
1886	Heinz Tomato Ketchup sold in Fortnum & Mason
1895	Heinz Baked Beans first sold
1910	Cream of Tomato Soup first sold in the UK
1925	Spaghetti added to the company's range
1938	Heinz Baby Food first sold
1946	Heinz Tomato Ketchup first manufactured in UK
1959	Kitt Green factory opened, Europe's largest food factory
1995	Heinz celebrates 100 years of Heinz Baked Beans
1996	Heinz celebrates 100 years of "57 Varieties"

The magic number "57"

In 1896 Henry Heinz spotted a shoe advertisement which read "21 styles". That set him totting up his own products; 56, 57, 58, 59... There were still a few more, but something made him linger on "57". It seemed a distinctive number, so "57 Varieties" it was. Today the worldwide business markets many hundreds of products under various brand names, but the famous "57 Varieties" trademark has passed into the language.

Contents

Animal Encounters

Look! Look! Look!

The Great Outdoors

Somewhat Historical

Up, Down, There & Back

The Sun Has Got His Hat On

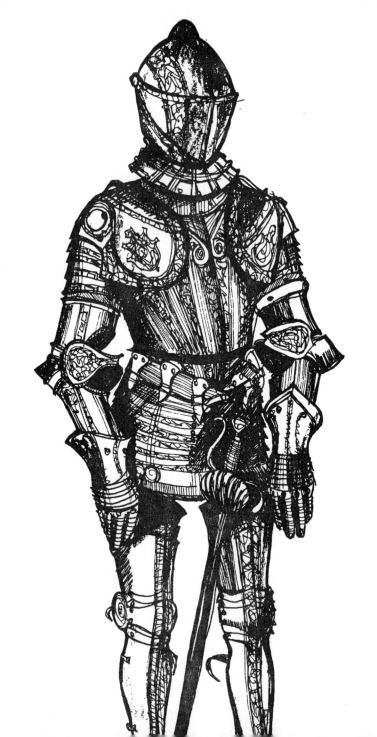

Introduction

Welcome to The Heinz Guide to Days Out With Kids, a book written for people with children in the West Country. Here in its second edition, you'll find it is packed with ideas for fun family outings. With lots of trips to try and up-to-date information for 1999/2000, I hope that it will help you tackle some of those perennial problems:

What Are We Going To Do Today?
As a mother of four children, I know how important it is to get out of the house some days. Equally, how difficult it can be to think of places to go for a change; places that are not too far; where everyone can have a good time; where young children will be well catered for. This book gives you a personal selection of great outings to choose from; if you go out on one or two a month, there are well over a year's worth of different trips inside!

But Where Is Really Good?
Often these days it is not a problem knowing about places to go, but rather whether those places will really be a good trip for people with children. If you've no time to sift through leaflets, or don't know anyone who's been themselves then it can be daunting to try something new. The outings featured in The Heinz Guide to Days Out With Kids have all been done personally, by mothers with children in tow. They are all tried-and-tested recommended trips: we've been there ourselves!

What about Mums And Dads too?
If the prospect of yet another adventure playground bores you, then you'll welcome something different. Our aim has been to describe outings enjoyed by everyone in the family, with something to appeal to adults as well as children. Some of the trips may look like just adult outings, but they're not. We want to introduce you to some of the unusual and fun places we have been to. You may all get something different out of the day, but that doesn't matter, as long as you all have a good time.

How Are Places Selected For The Book?

We have included a variety of trips: for the winter and the summer, for rain and sunshine, some nearby, some a greater distance. Some of the trips are old favourites, many times visited. Others were suggested by friends as places that they love. We have noted what childcare facilities are provided in each case: pushchair accessibility, high chairs, nappy tables etc., but haven't selected places purely on this basis. Rather, the facilities information is given on the principle that if you know in advance what is provided you can plan your day accordingly.

All trips were done anonymously. No one has paid to be included in the book, and the views and opinions expressed are very much personal thoughts and reactions. Places are in the book because we had a good time there, and think that other people with children could too.

What Ages Of Children Are Covered?

The book is aimed at people with babies, toddlers and school-aged children. Many of the trips will also appeal to children up to early teens and, of course, adults too! The facts given for each outing have been checked rigorously. However, things do change, and please check details (particularly opening times) before you set out.

Special Events?

Finally, our new web site is currently under development. Check it out on **www.daysoutwithkids.co.uk** for extra information on special events and the like.

Janet Bonthron
Series Editor
Bon•Bon Ventures
24 Endlesham Road
London SW12 8JU

How To Use This Book

EACH SECTION OF THE BOOK COVERS TRIPS WHICH FALL INTO THE same broad category of attraction. Outings are described alphabetically within the section. If you know what sort of outing you want to do, then just look at the section titles, read the section summaries below and flick through the entries included in that section. Alternatively, the handy planning guide is a rapid, self-explanatory table for identifying the right trip for you.

ANIMAL ENCOUNTERS covers trips to farms, zoos and other birds-and-beasties type places. Children and animals are a winning combination, and there are plenty of places around the West Country which offer it. We have chosen those which we think are distinctive in some way, for example, superb handling opportunities for children, wonderful setting, or unusual or imaginatively-displayed animals. Try them all for variety!

LOOK! LOOK! LOOK! features places with exhibitions or displays which children should particularly enjoy, be they science-based (The Exploratory or Techniquest), wild birds and birds of prey (Slimbridge or the National Birds of Prey Centre), or a full-sized sailing ship (SS Great Britain). These outings offer the chance for children to see something unusual or to experience at close quarters something they may only have seen on television.

THE GREAT OUTDOORS is about trips which are all or mostly outdoors in character, in an especially beautiful or quiet setting. Ideal for walks and strolls, with plenty to see for adults whilst the little horrors run around exhausting themselves. Couldn't be better!

SOMEWHAT HISTORICAL attractions all have a bygone age theme. Your children may not fully appreciate the historical connotations, but will be able to enjoy the setting and exhibits, whilst you can wallow in romantic nostalgia!

UP, DOWN, THERE & BACK has steam train outings. Puffs of steam and the smell of smoke in the air are always thrilling and the ones we have included have features which make them particularly accessible. Eat your heart out, Thomas the Tank Engine!

THE SUN HAS GOT HIS HAT ON includes picnic spots that are obviously just a small selection of what is available. Most good picnic spots tend to be closely guarded secrets, but these are ones which are favourites of ours. There is something about spreading your blanket on the ground and unpacking boxes and plates of picnic food that is just pure summertime, and you can't beat it. Happy munching! Of course, many of the locations in the previous sections are also excellent picnic spots.

IF YOU DON'T MIND WHAT SORT OF ATTRACTION YOU GO TO, BUT HAVE other criteria (such as the weather, distance, or means of transport, for example) which you need to satisfy, then the best way to use the book is to refer to the map and planning guide given on the following pages. These should help you to pick a suitable day out.

THE PLANNING GUIDE can help you select an outing by distance, prevailing weather, admittance to dogs, accessibility by public transport or opening hours. * **Free**, or particularly **good value**, trips are asterisked (less than about £10 for a family of four).

Distances are approximate, and taken from Bristol. We have erred on the generous side when deciding on the **wet weather** suitability – if there is somewhere to duck inside during an occasional shower then we say 'yes' under the wet weather trip heading. 'No' means, in our view, it would really be quite a miserable trip if it is raining. For people with dogs, 'yes' may mean on a lead only, so always take a lead.

With **public transport** accessibility we have indicated what is available, but you may need to do a short walk too in some cases. 'None' or 'limited' means that it would really be hard work going there without a car.

The planning guide also indicates whether **opening** periods are restricted (i.e. if a place is not open all the year, and/or only on some days of the week). For attractions cited as 'all year' opening, this excludes Christmas Day, Boxing Day and New Year's Day, so check if you want to go these days.

Once you have identified a trip that sounds appealing, refer to the detailed description for further information. Page numbers are given in the Planning Guide. The Fact File which accompanies each entry gives the address and telephone number, travel directions and distances, opening times and prices and an indication of specific facilities (high chairs, nappy change areas and eating places). Where appropriate, the Fact File also suggests other nearby attractions.

Map

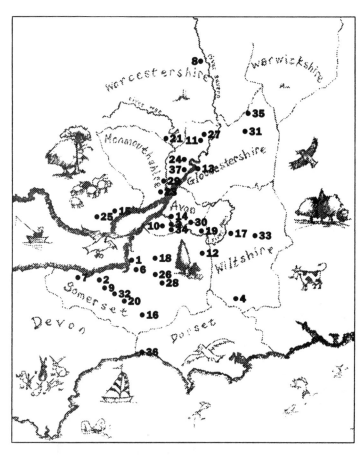

PLANNING GUIDE

OUTING	DISTANCE (MILES)	WET WEATHER TRIP	DOGS	PUBLIC TRANSPORT	OPEN	PAGE
ANIMAL ENCOUNTERS						
ANIMAL FARM COUNTRY PARK	30	NO	NO	BUS	ALL YEAR	15
BEE WORLD AND ANIMAL CENTRE	50	YES	NO	TRAIN	RESTRICTED	18
BRISTOL ZOOLOGICAL GARDENS	2	YES	NO	BUS	ALL YEAR	21
FARMER GILES FARMSTEAD	90	NO	YES	NONE	RESTRICTED	24
HEAVEN'S GATE ANIMAL SANCTUARY *	55	NO	NO	NONE	RESTRICTED	27
SECRET WORLD BADGER & WILDLIFE RESCUE CENTRE	25	NO	NO	NONE	ALL YEAR	30
TROPIQUARIA	55	YES	NO	BUS	RESTRICTED	33
WEST MIDLAND SAFARI PARK	70	YES	NO	NONE	RESTRICTED	36
LOOK! LOOK! LOOK!						
BLAZES MUSEUM *	60	YES	NO	BUS	RESTRICTED	39
THE EXPLORATORY	0	YES	NO	TRAIN	ALL YEAR	42
THE NATIONAL BIRDS OF PREY CENTRE	38	NO	NO	NONE	RESTRICTED	45
RODE BIRD GARDENS	30	NO	NO	BUS	ALL YEAR	48
SLIMBRIDGE WILDFOWL & WETLAND CENTRE	25	YES	NO	BUS	ALL YEAR	51
SS GREAT BRITAIN & MARITIME HERITAGE CENTRE	2	YES	NO	BUS & FERRY	ALL YEAR	54
TECHNIQUEST	60	YES	NO	BUS	ALL YEAR	57
THE GREAT OUTDOORS						
BARRINGTON COURT GARDENS	50	NO	NO	NONE	RESTRICTED	60
BOWOOD HOUSE	15	NO	NO	BUS	RESTRICTED	63
CHEDDAR GORGE	30	YES	NO	BUS	ALL YEAR	66
DYRHAM PARK *	12	NO	NO	BUS	RESTRICTED	69
HESTERCOMBE GARDENS *	45	NO	NO	NONE	ALL YEAR	72
JUBILEE MAZE *	45	YES	NO	NONE	RESTRICTED	75
WESTONBIRT ARBORETUM *	35	NO	YES	NONE	ALL YEAR	78

OUTING	DISTANCE (MILES)	WET WEATHER TRIP	DOGS	PUBLIC TRANSPORT	OPEN	PAGE
SOMEWHAT HISTORICAL						
CHEPSTOW CASTLE & MUSEUM*	15	YES	NO	LIMITED	ALL YEAR	81
CLEARWELL CAVES *	40	YES	NO	NONE	RESTRICTED	84
MUSEUM OF WELSH LIFE	50	YES	YES	BUS	ALL YEAR	87
PEAT MOORS IRON AGE VISITOR CENTRE *	55	YES	NO	NONE	RESTRICTED	90
SHAMBLES MUSEUM *	40	YES	YES	NONE	RESTRICTED	93
SOMERSET RURAL LIFE MUSEUM*	40	YES	NO	BUS	RESTRICTED	96
TINTERN ABBEY & OLD STATION*	20	NO	NO	BUS	ALL YEAR	99
UP, DOWN, THERE AND BACK						
AVON VALLEY RAILWAY *	5	YES	YES	BUS	RESTRICTED	102
THE GLOUCESTERSHIRE & WARWICKSHIRE RAILWAY	55	YES	YES	BUS	RESTRICTED	105
WEST SOMERSET RAILWAY	60	YES	YES	BUS	RESTRICTED	108
THE SUN HAS GOT HIS HAT ON						
AVEBURY STONE CIRCLE *	30	NO	YES	BUS	ALL YEAR	111
AVON VALLEY COUNTRY PARK	5	NO	NO	BUS	RESTRICTED	114
BROADWAY TOWER COUNTRY PARK *	50	NO	YES	BUS	RESTRICTED	117
CHARMOUTH BEACH *	80	NO	NO	NONE	ALL YEAR	120
FOREST OF DEAN SCULPTURE TRAIL *	50	NO	YES	NONE	ALL YEAR	123

SEE **HOW TO USE THIS GUIDE** FOR EXPLANATIONS

Animal Encounters

Animal Farm Country Park

"A farmer's life for me"

SAVE THIS ONE FOR A DAY WHEN EVERYONE IS FEELING FULL OF energy and raring to go, because this is one day out that really needs a whole day. And choose a fine one so that you can take your time in good weather to enjoy all of the park.

Animal Farm Country Park has everything to ensure a busy, fun-filled outing with all the things you'd expect to find in a well-run family attraction:

"Lots of animals ready for a stroke or a cuddle"

lots of animals eager to be fed and always ready for a stroke or a cuddle, and plenty of play areas with opportunities galore for climbing, swinging, bouncing and jumping.

The first thing to do as you enter the park is to buy some bags of feed, 35p a bag and well worth investing in for the entertainment they provide. Clutching their bags, our children excitedly ran off to the first animals they could find – friendly goats who were more than happy to eat the food they were offered – before moving on to the pigs next door who willingly emerged from their cool mudbaths to trot obligingly towards the handfuls of food held out to them. Pigs and children were all delighted.

What was left of the food when the goats and pigs had finished was liberally distributed around the

neighbouring rabbit hutches.

Nearby are several play areas, catering for a wide range of ages. The small slide was perfect for our toddler while the older children raced up and down a larger one close by. There are two shutes so there should not be too many bottlenecks. There is also an indoor play barn for under-fives where you'll find all the essentials . . . soft play and a ball pool, and an indoor area for picnics, essential in wet weather but just as useful in high summer.

The Cuddle Club was the favourite part of our visit though. It is in one of the barns and gives everyone

SAM

the chance to stroke and feed the smaller animals. There
are seats for the children to sit on and then they're given
a rabbit, a guinea pig or a white rat to stroke (each on a
square of carpet to avoid 'accidents'!). There are also
baby birds on hand for a pat, though the staff keep hold
of them. It proved so popular with our troops that they
had to be persuaded with a Cuddle Club sticker to give
up their places to others waiting for a turn.

If energy levels have been restored, you can head
straight outside again to the three big round trampolines
– large enough for half a dozen small people at a time.
Every child seems to have an in-built desire to bounce
and a session on these trampolines saves the bed springs
at least for a day!

Finish off by following the signs to the paddock from
where you can go on a leisurely and very tranquil half-
hour walk through field after field of animals, from the
expected (sheep) to the unexpected (a llama). The walk is
a circular one so you'll find yourselves back at the play
areas.

Fact File

- ADDRESS: Animal Farm Country Park, Red Road, Berrow, near Burnham-on-Sea, Somerset
- TELEPHONE: 01278 751628
- DIRECTIONS: M5 to junction 22, then follow brown tourist signs
- PUBLIC TRANSPORT: Bus 112 from Weston-super-Mare and Burnham-on-Sea
- DISTANCE: 30 miles
- TRAVEL TIME : 45 minutes
- OPENING: 10.00am-5.30pm (4.00pm winter)
- PRICES: Adults £3.75, children £3.00, under-3's free
- RESTAURANT FACILITIES: Yes
- NAPPY CHANGING FACILITIES: Yes
- HIGH CHAIRS: Yes
- DOGS: No
- PUSHCHAIR FRIENDLY: Yes
- NEARBY: 1 mile from beach at Brean Sands

Bee World and Animal Centre

IN A LOVELY SETTING ON THE EDGE OF THE QUANTOCK HILLS, BEE World and Animal Centre lies snugly between the West Somerset Railway line and the Doniford Brook, a mile from the village of Stogumber. The centre has been carefully planned to provide an exceptional variety of interest – make sure your first stop is a check on the day's timetable posted on a blackboard in the barn, to make sure you don't miss any opportunity for face-to-face encounters with the various animals.

You can get your bearings if you start out, as we did, with an enjoyable walk around the farm's boundary; past the ornamental lake where moorhens drift, waterlilies float and enormous koi carp swim; alongside pasture for goats, sheep and cattle and on through wild flower meadows. All the way is on beautifully mown paths: easy walking for children's small feet and smooth running for buggies and wheelchairs. The path follows the river bank along its meandering course and the way is punctuated by tables and benches, some in leafy shady spots and others out in the sunshine, where you can picnic or simply take time out. The river itself provides a wonderful natural play area for the more adventurous children to scramble on to the pebble beaches and paddle in the cool water. But don't take your eyes off them. The river bank is steep in places and the water fast flowing.

"The whole bee story is told with working displays of bees and wasps, combs, hives, honey and candles"

At the bottom of the main events field where pony rides are given, 50p a time (or £1 for the larger pony), there is a terrific adventure play area which includes one of the most exciting and original swings we'd ever seen.

You could stay here all day, but we continued back towards the farm, past the lake and the rare breeds field to the piggery and the enchanting pygmy goats. Many of the animals are brought in to the covered barn during the day to give visitors a chance to get close and chat to Honky the donkey and Eric and Ernie the Shetland ponies or feed lambs and calves. Our children chose to get closer still, spending a long half an hour cuddling the rabbits and guinea pigs.

The entrance to Bee World itself is nearby. Here you'll find the whole bee story told with working displays of bees and wasps (behind glass!), combs, hives, honey and candles. Try to spot the queen in the observation hive, shiver in fascinated horror at the hornets' and wasps' nests (not occupied, thankfully), and, on some days, marvel as the products are extracted from the working hives right in front of your eyes. You are able to see wax products being made and can buy them and other bee-related products in the shop at the entrance. There's

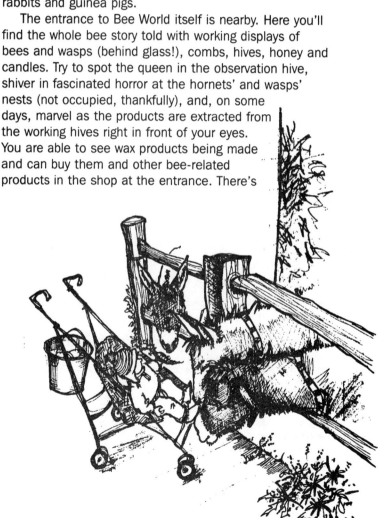

☞ even a great floor puzzle for smaller visitors to do while their grown-ups have a good look round. Finally, don't miss the screen in the video centre showing live pictures of bee-keeping and other goings-on around the farm.

Alongside is a play area: a fenced lawn with a wonderful old tractor to climb all over, toddler swings and the biggest sandpit most children will ever see! The children insisted that we sit at one of the picnic tables here until a steam train passed so they could wave at it. Happily there was one along quite quickly.

Bee World and Animal Centre is such a relaxed and happy place that once you've discovered it, you'll be back again and again. See you there.

Fact File

- ADDRESS: Bee World and Animal Centre, Stogumber Station, Stogumber, Somerset
- TELEPHONE: 01984 656545
- DIRECTIONS: A358 Taunton to Minehead road. Follow brown tourist signs at Crowcombe/Stogumber crossroads
- PUBLIC TRANSPORT: West Somerset Railway from Minehead or Bishops Lydeard
- DISTANCE: 50 miles
- TRAVEL TIME: 1 hour 30 minutes via Williton
- OPENING: Easter to end October, 10.00am-6.00pm or dusk
- PRICES: Adults £3.30, 5-16 years £2.30, 2-4 years 70p, under-2's free
- RESTAURANT FACILITIES: Yes
- NAPPY CHANGING FACILITIES: Yes
- HIGH CHAIRS: Yes
- DOGS: No
- PUSHCHAIR-FRIENDLY: Yes
- NEARBY: Coombe Sydenham walks, Torre Cider Washford

Bristol Zoological Gardens

"Cats and rats and elephants and chimpanzees"

FORGET ANY PRECONCEPTIONS AND PREJUDICES ABOUT ZOOS – Bristol Zoo is a very special place and it offers an incredible range of activities for the family. The minute you walk into the impressive entrance hall to the Gardens you can feel you're in for a treat and what follows doesn't disappoint. Look out for the new penguin and seal exhibition, opening in summer 1999, where you can see them feeding and swimming underwater.

Everywhere you can see the evidence of real imagination and flair in the way the animals are housed and presented to the visitor – the monkey house in particular is a triumph. We were transfixed, watching them cavort around in their outdoor homes, but we all thought it was even better when we walked round the back into the Monkey House

"There are few animals which exert the same fascination as a family of chimpanzees relaxing at home doing a bit of nit-picking"

itself and had a glimpse of their home life through glass walls: it was mesmerising. There really are few animals which can exert the same fascination as a family of chimpanzees relaxing at home indulging in a spot of nit-picking . . . it's all in the way they're so like us and at the same time not like us at all!

Once we'd laughed our way through the Monkey House, the lure of the new adventure playground proved too much for the children and we had a picnic there while the kids played. Parking ourselves at a table we unloaded while they raced off, the more confident of the two boys to ape the monkey tricks he'd just witnessed while the other headed straight for the bouncy castle. A bit steep at 50p for five minutes, but when he elected to come off after five seconds the 50p was refunded voluntarily. When the picnic debris had been packed away and ice-lollies were happily dripping down little hands, a vote was taken and we headed for the small mammal house.

It's in the special exhibitions that Bristol Zoo really comes into its own – within the small mammal house is a reconstruction of a section of a real house, complete with tiny inhabitants. The mouse in the breadbin was a touch disconcerting but had nothing on the writhing jumble in the washing machine that never showed its face! This idea is repeated in Bug World where a loo is home to a

spider and you can get right inside a desert scene containing more locusts than you'd care to meet in the raw. I crawled inside to have a look but I reckon it's better if you're only three feet tall. Twilight World is also brilliantly presented with bark chippings underfoot deadening sound so as not to disturb these nocturnal creatures – we were quite convinced we were walking along the forest floor. The Aquarium is home to a quite dazzling variety of fish, from the drop dead ugly to the quite extravagantly beautiful, and from the very tiny to the unbelievably big.

If the adventure playground isn't sufficient entertainment when the animal attractions threaten to pall, there is also an activity centre for children, where kids can have their faces painted (this explains the herds of small human animals running around), or try their hands at brass rubbing.

There's only one drawback to Bristol Zoo and that's the parking; it's very limited and if you don't arrive early you could find yourself in for a bit of a walk. You have been warned.

Fact File

- ADDRESS: Bristol Zoo Gardens, Clifton, Bristol, Avon
- TELEPHONE: 0117 973 8951 (24hr information line)
- DIRECTIONS: M5 to junction 17/18, then follow brown tourist signs. Also signposted from city centre
- PUBLIC TRANSPORT: British Rail to Bristol Templemeads, then bus 8,9, 508, or 509
- DISTANCE: 2 miles
- TRAVEL TIME: 15 minutes
- OPENING: Daily 9.00am-5.30pm (summer), 4.30pm (winter)
- PRICES: Adults £7.95, children £4.50, under-3's free
- RESTAURANT FACILITIES: Yes
- NAPPY CHANGING FACILITIES: Yes
- HIGH CHAIRS: Yes
- DOGS: No
- PUSHCHAIR-FRIENDLY: Yes
- NEARBY: Ashton Court 0117 963 9174

Farmer Giles Farmstead

"Eey-aie-eeh-aie-oh!"

DRESSED IN WELLIES AND MUFFLED UP FIRMLY AGAINST THE AUTUMN wind, we set off for a day on the farm at Farmer Giles Farmstead. Now veteran farm visitors, the children knew the drill, so as we entered the farm through the particularly well-stocked gift shop they bought their bags of feed and set off eagerly in search of the animals. The goats were first and were happy – as goats everywhere are – to scoff what was offered and nuzzle up our sleeves for more.

The Farmstead is a working farm with lots of activities taking place all day – we immediately made a note of milking time (2.30pm daily) as it was something none of us had seen before! My daughter was on a rabbit-cuddling mission, though. We found what she was looking for in a barn where the children can sit surrounded by straw and rabbits, stroking

"Lambs could compete very successfully in a beer-drinking contest"

and cuddling to their hearts' content. Outside in the yard again, we spotted the tractor with its trailer stacked with bales of hay ready to do a tour round the farm. These run daily at 1.30pm and 2.30pm and cost 50p per person, though extra rides will be put on if there is demand for more.

While you are waiting you can have a go at donkey grooming or bottle-feeding the lambs. We set off for the lambs – beware! Lambs could compete very successfully in a beer-drinking contest. They clamp on to the teat and are determined to drain the contents in one. Our two-year-old wasn't expecting this and was a bit worried by the grip on 'his' bottle while our daughter lost her hold halfway through and her bottle smashed. It's best to hover close by and give little ones a helping hand.

Calm was restored by the mention of lunch which we ate in The Old Barn Restaurant: simple, traditional home-cooked food at extremely reasonable prices. If you bring a picnic, you'll find both indoor and outdoor picnic areas available.

After lunch it was time for the long-awaited ride on a trailer packed with other families. The tractor slowly pulled us all up a steep hillside field full of cows to give a breathtaking panoramic view of the farm and the countryside beyond. 'Farmer Giles' himself (?) climbed out of his tractor to answer children's questions about the farm; 'how many cows?' and 'don't they get cold in the winter?'. Then it's case of hold on tight for the alarming journey back down the hill.

Don't miss the hand-milking when you get back. An extremely patient Jersey cow allows all and sundry a go: some of us were more successful than others, it goes

without saying, but it made an unusual treat.

Run off any spare energy in the adventure playground – paradise for my four-year-old who could have stayed all day climbing, sliding and jumping, but a little tricky for the two-year-old who scooted off to explore the tractors nearby. These proved to be a little boy's dream: he climbed on and off them endlessly, turning the steering wheel and fiddling with every available lever, in a world of his own.

With animals, animals and more animals as well as tractors, tractors and more tractors for a tractor-mad boy, Farmer Giles made the perfect (and very hands-on) day out. As we left, I quietly made a note of the weekends in December when Father Christmas will be visiting – won't they be surprised to find him down on the farm?

Fact File

- ADDRESS: Farmer Giles Farmstead, Teffont, Salisbury, Wiltshire
- TELEPHONE: 01722 716338
- DIRECTIONS: M5 to junction 25, then A358 to Ilminster and A303 to Teffont, then follow brown tourist signs
- PUBLIC TRANSPORT: No
- DISTANCE: 90 miles
- TRAVEL TIME: 1 hour 40 minutes
- OPENING: Daily 10.00am-6.00pm, March 21st to November 8th. Weekends in the winter
- PRICES: Adults £3.95, children £2.85, under-2's free. Family £13.00
- RESTAURANT FACILITIES: Yes
- NAPPY CHANGING FACILITIES: Yes
- HIGH CHAIRS: Yes
- DOGS: Yes
- PUSHCHAIR-FRIENDLY: Yes
- NEARBY: Stonehenge, Salisbury Cathedral

Heaven's Gate Farm

"How much is that doggy in the window?"

HEAVEN'S GATE FARM IS PROBABLY OUR FAMILY'S FAVOURITE DAY OUT – it's open all year round and has lots of special Fun Days as well, with dog shows and plenty of other entertainment.

Set in 25 acres of idyllic countryside overlooking Kings Sedgemoor, this is a wonderful place to visit to escape the hustle and bustle of city life. The farm is run by the National Animal Welfare Trust and is home to more than 200 animals: cats and dogs, hamsters and gerbils, turkeys and deer among them. Every time we visit we realise why we love it so much: it has such a unique atmosphere and we're always struck by the sense of everybody working hard for the animals and loving every minute of it.

A map of the farm is provided but this is a lovely place to just wander around at your own pace, going where the fancy – or the children – take you. Everywhere you go you'll find volunteers hard at work, cleaning, tidying and

"My two-year-old still performs his turkey impression for anyone willing to watch"

feeding the animals, but they're never too busy to stop and chat about the farm and the animals. If you're keen, they'll also happily accept any offers of help! In the course of our visit, our three-year-old enthusiastically set about helping to clear the weeds from some steps and later on was delighted to spot a guinea-pig's empty bowl which she was then invited to fill.

It's important to remember that the farm is home to a lot of dogs and the noise they make can be a bit alarming to small children – ours were a bit taken aback at the welcome they got as we approached but they were soon busy discovering what the dogs were all called and which of them were looking for new homes. We certainly

weren't thinking about taking a dog home but we all had good fun helping a family who had come especially to adopt a dog as they chose their new pet. Before they selected the lucky animal, a volunteer told them all about the dogs: how they'd come to be at Heaven's Gate; what they liked . . . and what they didn't; about their good habits . . . and their bad ones.

Make a detour to the cool, shady stables where you'll find two beautiful ponies standing patiently while children pat their velvety noses and stroke their necks. But the rabbits were the main attraction for us, all of them have a run and the children loved picking grass and feeding it through the wire to the waiting mouths. The grass was obviously greener on the other side of the wire because the rabbits sat on their bit of grass and pulled every last bit through and looked as if they'd have done it all day long.

But for our two-year-old son the rabbits were instantly forgotten when he discovered the two huge turkeys which 'gobbled' their way up and down the enclosure, staring us out and keeping pace as he raced up and down beside them. He still performs his turkey impression for anyone willing to watch and I think I'm going to have to rename the Christmas dinner this year!

As an escape from city life, Heaven's Gate lives up to its name . . . peaceful (away from the dogs!), beautifully situated and a real tonic. Try it yourselves.

Fact File

- ADDRESS: National Animal Welfare Trust (NAWT), Heaven's Gate Farm, West Henley, Langport, Somerset
- TELEPHONE: 01458 252656
- DIRECTIONS: M5 to junction 23, then the A39 Glastonbury road to Ashcott. Turn right at Albion pub, right at end of road on to Nythe Road, then follow signs to Animal Rescue Centre
- PUBLIC TRANSPORT: No
- DISTANCE: 55 miles
- TRAVEL TIME: 1 hour
- OPENING: 11.00am-3.30pm daily
- PRICES: Suggested donation £1.00
- RESTAURANT FACILITIES: Yes
- NAPPY CHANGING FACILITIES: No
- HIGH CHAIRS: No
- DOGS: No
- PUSHCHAIR-FRIENDLY: Yes
- NEARBY: Stembridge Windmill, High Ham or Eastfield Nature Reserve Turn Hill

Secret World Badger & Wildlife Rescue Centre

IF YOU WANT A DAY OUT WITH ANIMALS, BUT YOU'RE LOOKING FOR somewhere just a little bit different, look no further. At Secret World you'll find all the usual farm animals but the real attraction lies in the wild animals – especially badgers – that you're not normally lucky enough to see.

We visited Secret World on a warm summer's day and even before we arrived we'd thoroughly enjoyed the journey there through the beautiful Somerset levels. Once we arrived we discovered that we were going to have a packed day – a blackboard listed the day's events – milking, rabbit feeding, a meeting with a barn owl and lots more treats. We decided to save the farm animals for later and headed for the courtyard which is home to many secret worlds. Each doorway has a hidden world behind it: we were given a fascinating glimpse (behind glass) of a beehive in action but the favourite with our children was the hedgehog room where they were able to get really close to the hedgehogs. And when

"We couldn't resist the invitation to climb in and meet a field of sheep"

they've looked enough you'll find that a drawing table is thoughtfully provided alongside to let them draw their new friends.

Clutching hedgehog pictures, we all agreed it was time for lunch and set off for the farmhouse, a beautiful 17th century building where upstairs is home for the Kidners (who run Secret World) and downstairs has been converted to tea-rooms. Most impressive was the speed with which our food arrived – no time for a toddler to get impatient. Even during lunch the animals weren't far away: as we sat outside to eat, several hens played Hoover with whatever landed on the floor.

To discover the real secret of Secret World, follow the signs to the badgers. Inside a darkened shed you'll see a rare sight: four or five badgers curled comfortably around each other, all fast asleep. Badgers, foxes, owls and ferrets aside, Secret World is also home to plenty of the animals children are more used to – cows, pigs, rabbits, guinea pigs and goats – and we couldn't resist the invitation to climb in and meet a field of sheep.

Our homeward journey was delayed by the well-equipped play areas (tractors, tyres and cargo nets, swings, slides and sandpits). But what price a good night's sleep?

You used to be able to hire bikes at Secret World and follow the Bluebell Trail across country for a few miles. Sadly, you can

☞ no longer hire bikes there, but they are available from the nearby village of Burtle (on the Somerset Moors) which is also a point on the Bluebell Trail. So if you fancy a chance to see the countryside from a different perspective, and to cycle to Secret World from the village and back, simply turn up at the cycle hire shop (01278 722269) in the village instead. It will cost about £25 for a family of four to be kitted out with everything for the day. Several different types of bikes are available including tandems, trailers for kids and child seats, and helmets all round. It does make a really different day out: we hired two bikes with a trailer for the children and were relieved to find that the ride was flat. It's not a difficult ride, and takes about forty minutes to Secret World. The children were very taken with the novelty of riding in a trailer with Mum pulling them along!

Fact File

● ADDRESS: Secret World, New Road Farm, East Huntspill, near Highbridge, Somerset
● TELEPHONE: 01278 783250
● DIRECTIONS: M5 to junction 22 and follow brown tourist signs on A38 at West Huntspill
● PUBLIC TRANSPORT: None
● DISTANCE: 25 miles
● TRAVEL TIME: 40 minutes
● OPENING: Daily 10.00am-6.00pm (dusk if earlier). Closed in January
● PRICES: Adults £4.75, children £3.50, family £15.00, under-3's free
● RESTAURANT FACILITIES: Yes
● NAPPY CHANGING FACILITIES: Yes
● HIGH CHAIRS: Yes
● DOGS: No
● PUSHCHAIR-FRIENDLY: Yes
● NEARBY: Numerous cycle trails and cycle hire facilities (01278 722269) from Burtle

Tropiquaria

"Along came a spider and sat down beside her"

HOUSED IN THE UNUSUAL AND UNEXPECTED SETTING OF A REDUNDANT radio transmitting station, Tropiquaria is West Somerset's wildlife park and much, much more as well, offering an exciting day out for anyone of any age.

Here you can have a snake draped around your neck and hold a tarantula in the palm of your hand (should you want to!). I declined both offers but the children were surprisingly eager to have a go. Some of them found it challenging and even a little bit frightening but were thrilled by the experience and really proud to have done it. What a great way to deal with potential phobias.

We wandered into Tropical Hall where a perfect simulation of the tropical climate is maintained, allowing children to discover exactly what the natural habitat of the animals would be like. You can follow the board walk

> ## "Have a snake draped around your neck or hold a tarantula in the palm of your hand"

around the exhibits, marvelling at all the amazing and colourful creatures: iguanas and geckos, the American basilisk, various snakes, snapping turtles, spiders, alligators and a variety of birds, all living free in their indoor jungle. Then continue downstairs through the aquarium to see piranhas, anemones and the extraordinary cow fish among a multitude of exotic and magical sea creatures on display.

Outside again, we headed for the picnic and play area immediately in front of the building. Here turkeys and pot-bellied pigs wandered around the tables Hoovering the grass as I relaxed with a cup of coffee and the children ran off to the trampolines, the obstacle course and the enormous sandpit. There are the lemur garden, the

chipmunks' run, the wallabies' extensive paddock, the owls and kookaburras, the jays, ibis and cranes all waiting to be discovered. Not to mention the most incredible adventure playfort with an adjacent picnic area of its own. My children played happily here for ages – it's a day out in itself so it is well worth planning to spend a good length of time here.

Back inside, there is the Parrot's Perch restaurant, where we had a long conversation with a huge blue and yellow macaw in the entrance hall, and the shop with a wealth of reasonably priced merchandise. If you're caught short by a shower or visit on a rainy day you'll no doubt welcome the video and indoor picnic room too.

Finally there is the Shadowstring Puppet Theatre. Performing at least three times a day in the summer holidays, their fantastic shows should not be missed. For all of us this was the highlight of the day. Bright lights, clever staging, brilliant puppeteering, hilarious songs and altogether a great deal of fun. So when you hear the bell that heralds the start of the show, hurry in, get a good seat and settle down for a special treat.

With everything Tropiquaria has to offer I was bowled over by the quality of the day out we had there – if you're in this area or even if you're not, don't miss it.

Fact File

- ADDRESS: Tropiquaria, Washford Cross, Watchet, Somerset
- TELEPHONE: 01984 640688
- DIRECTIONS: M5 to junction 23 or junction 25, then A358 to Minehead. A39 between Williton and Minehead (look out for the tall radio masts)
- PUBLIC TRANSPORT: Bus 28 and 15 (from Bridgewater, Taunton or Minehead)
- DISTANCE: 55 miles
- TRAVEL TIME: 1 hour 30 minutes from Bristol via Williton
- OPENING: Daily 10.00am-5.00pm, Easter to mid-September, and 11.00am-4.00pm, mid-September to end October. Weekends and school holidays 11.00am-dusk in November, February & March
- PRICES: Adults £4.40, children £2.95, under-3's free
- RESTAURANT FACILITIES: Yes
- NAPPY CHANGING FACILITIES: Yes
- HIGH CHAIRS: No
- DOGS: No
- PUSHCHAIR-FRIENDLY: Yes
- NEARBY: Torre Cider Washford or Aquasplash wave pool, Dunster

West Midland Safari & Leisure Park

ONE DAY DOESN'T SEEM ENOUGH TO SEE AND DO ALL THAT THERE IS here, so leave yourself plenty of time. Getting in can be a slow process on a busy day, but as we waited there were already squeals of delight coming from the back of the car as camels were spotted on the horizon. This set the tone for the next 90 minutes' journey through the wild lands of three continents, with shouts of "Look, tigers!" or "Mummy, zebras!" whenever we went over the next hill or round the next bend.

The Park is split into African, American and Eurasian sections and within these are areas where you can drive with your car windows open. There are even some areas where you can feed the animals through your open window. There are, however, other areas where opening your windows is definitely not allowed. Make sure you do a toilet stop before you start, too.

"A friendly camel put his head inside the car to say hello"

Past camels, zebras and elands, we entered a 'windows closed' section, where a sign tells you that monkeys WILL damage cars. At this point you are offered an alternative route, but we risked it. Immediately, monkeys appeared, as if from nowhere, scampering all around and climbing on bonnets and roofs. Our car may be old, but we were glad it didn't have its window seals nibbled like the car in front did!

Having survived the attention of the monkeys, the lions were next. As you go through electronically controlled double gates there is a feeling of adventure, and the adrenaline flows as you realise that you will be separated from the lions only by your car door. It feels uncanny to be braking to avoid a lioness wandering across the road, but for children, it is a marvellous opportunity to come face to face with what they have so far seen only in picture books.

After the perils of the monkeys and lions, we opened the car windows again to be greeted by a friendly camel, who put his head inside to say hello. The children loved it, but mummy was a bit startled to almost have a face wash from a large tongue!

Then came rhinoceroses, zebras, cows with enormous horns (Ankole Cattle) and peacocks (actually emus, but our children had never seen an emu before).

Another treat was the tigers, who decided to have an argument as we drove past and were roaring and running around. We were grateful here that the tigers were enclosed; monkeys on the roof is one thing, but angry tigers . . . ?

"Bambi's daddy!" shouted the children as we entered the final drive-through section. Here, the deer roam freely and are quick to put their heads into the car in search of food. If you want to make the most of this, be sure to buy a packet of food (80p) as you enter the Park, but be prepared! They are determined and it was difficult to drive

☞ away once they had got their head inside the car.

The rest of the Park is a fun fair and an area more like a traditional zoo, with a reptile house, monkeys in cages and an animal encounters area. The crocodiles and alligators in the reptile house were a magnet for our kids, with their glass-walled pools enabling you to see them moving amongst the fish.

Plan to see the sea-lions' act: four times a day in a specially built arena. There is also a parrot performance. The hippo feeding at 2.00pm is a riot: you can peer down at these lumbering giants from a viewing platform above the lake as they chomp their way through whole cabbages and the like. There are amusement rides to suit all ages, from gentle roundabouts to the stomach-churning pirate ship. Rides are an extra charge and you can buy a multi-ride wrist band (£6.25) or buy individual tickets. There are several fast food kiosks and cafeterias.

It wasn't until we were driving home that a voice from the back of the car reminded us: "We didn't go on the train". Yes, we had missed the Safari Express which gives a (free) ride around the leisure park. But when you go in you are given a FREE return ticket to the Park. We'll definitely be using ours!

Fact File

● ADDRESS: West Midland Safari & Leisure Park, Spring Grove, Bewdley, Worcestershire
● TELEPHONE: 01299 404604
● DIRECTIONS: M5 junction 6 and A449 to Kidderminster. From there follow the A456 towards Bewdley. Signposted
● PUBLIC TRANSPORT: None
● DISTANCE: 70 miles
● TRAVEL TIME: 1 hour 30 minutes
● OPENING: 20 March to end October daily 10.00-4.00pm (5.00pm weekends)
● PRICES: £5.25 per person, under-4's free. Includes free return visit
● RESTAURANT FACILITIES: Yes
● NAPPY CHANGING FACILITIES: Yes
● HIGH CHAIRS: Yes
● DOGS: No, bookable kennels available
● PUSHCHAIR-FRIENDLY: Yes
● NEARBY: Bewdley's 18th century Butchers' market and museum, with craft demonstrations. Wrye Forest, west of Bewdley, with waymarked walks and trails

Look! Look! Look!

Blazes Museum

"Ladybird, ladybird fly away home
Your house is on fire and your
children are gone!"

YOU'LL FIND THIS NEW MUSEUM IN SANDHILL PARK HOUSE ON THE edge of Somerset's beautiful and picturesque Quantock Hills. The house itself was built in 1720 on land once owned by King Alfred of Wessex and has been used as a hospital for much of its post-Victorian history. But now it's home to a host of fascinating fire-related paraphernalia, looking at fire from every possible angle. Fire's been

"The children donned helmets and operated the old-fashioned hand pumps"

with us a long time as friend and foe and here you'll find an exhibition guaranteed to spark the imagination of all those small children whose greatest ambition when they grow up is to be a fireman (sorry, firefighter). There's fire in nature, there's ways of making fire, fighting fire, preventing fire. And there's lots about the traditions and myths that surround fire. Any child who's seen *Jungle Book* knows just how valuable fire can be – 'what I desire is man's red fire'. The story is as old as time itself.

It's a well-designed and successfully executed exhibition – you're led round it by a friendly, fire-breathing, of course, dragon who points the way with his tongues of flame. Sometimes you'll find yourself in danger of forgetting the exhibition and simply admiring

the huge doorways and capacious passageways of
the building itself and reading the thoughtfully-
provided history of the house.

We entered the museum under a pictorial arch of
flame and accepted the invitation to sit and watch a
video introducing us to both the house and the exhibition.
The children loved the sense of being at the cinema,
while I was really pleased to find the house included as
well. The children were almost more interested in seeing
where the dragon took them next than in looking at
what's on display and were happy to take a quick look
and race on. But if they're happy and you're interested,
there really is lots here to look at and loads to discover,
with literally thousands of intriguing exhibits. If the
children stop for long enough, there's also lots of hands-
on experiences for them to enjoy, including an interactive
computer programme about fire-fighting.

We decided we would brave the optional, walk-through
son-et-lumiere display telling the story of the great fire of
Tooley Street in London which proved an exciting way to
discover just how fast fire can take hold. Even though you
know you're safe it's a sobering reminder of how fierce an
enemy fire is, and you might want to give this display a

miss if you've got really little ones with you.

The real treat of the trip for the children, though, was the old fire engines outside which, to their huge delight, they were allowed to clamber into and sit in the front seats. Then, better still, they were allowed to don the helmets (have a camera handy) and operate the old-fashioned hand pumps that were used in the infancy of fire-fighting. This bit of our visit (and the appearance of Fireman Sam everywhere in the shop) was a dream come true. Blazes is still very new and they've apparently got lots of plans for the museum: but already it's very impressive with exceptionally friendly and well-informed staff. We're all really looking forward to see what they do next . . .

Fact File

- ADDRESS: Blazes Museum, Sandhill Park, Bishops Lydeard, Taunton, Somerset
- TELEPHONE: 01823 433964
- DIRECTIONS: M5 to junction 25, just off A358 and close to Bishops Lydeard steam railway station
- PUBLIC TRANSPORT: Buses from Taunton and steam trains from Minehead
- DISTANCE: 60 miles
- TRAVEL TIME: 1 hour 30 minutes
- OPENING: Easter weekend, then 2 May to 24 October 10.00am-5.00pm. Closed Mondays (except Bank Holidays) and Saturdays
- PRICES: Adults £3.90, children £2.30, family £11.00, under-5's free
- RESTAURANT FACILITIES: Yes
- NAPPY CHANGING FACILITIES: No
- HIGH CHAIRS: No
- DOGS: No
- PUSHCHAIR-FRIENDLY: Yes
- NEARBY: Sheppy's Cider Museum (01823 461233) and the Quantock Hills

The Exploratory

MAKE SURE YOU CATCH THIS EXCELLENT MUSEUM BEFORE IT CLOSES in Autumn 1999. If you don't want to leave the city or it's raining cats and dogs but the children are desperate for entertainment, head for Bristol Old Station at Temple Meads (next door to the present station) and you'll find yourselves at The Exploratory, Bristol's hands-on science centre. Pre-schoolers of course don't understand the concept of science, but they're heavily into why and how and anything that does the unexpected. And they'll certainly find food for thought here. It's a place with a Heath Robinson feel to it: see something here and try it on your own at home.

We walked up to the door along the disused railway tracks, which provided the first excitement of the day and once inside our four-year-old was jumping up and down with impatience to be where the action was. His attention was immediately grabbed by someone making giant bubbles with special bubblemaking apparatus – forget the little pot and wand from the toyshop, these are serious bubbles! As the largest bubble of all time burst in front him, he was quickly diverted by the sight of a father and son apparently

"You can learn all about electricity, sound and lasers"

riding bicycles side by side while watching television. In fact they were pedalling furiously to see how much electricity they could generate – the TV was easy, just try getting the electric train to move!

The new Body Lab which opened last year is amazing. It's a permanent gallery where you can find out all about the workings of your own body. Wow! There's the chance to take body pieces out of life-sized model lying on an operating table – and can you fit them back in the right places? (It puts normal jigsaws into the pale.) Fiddle around with Skully the skeleton to learn about what's inside you, investigate how your heart works and try matching, with a hand-held pump, the heart pumping blood around the body after various activities. Then, go over to the Model Faces exhibition where you can have a go at a police-style computerised 'photofit' face reconstruction.

I tried to persuade the rest of the party to come with me to touch a tornado, but our son was far more interested in the Aladdin's Cave of a shop. With a promise of a visit as we left we persuaded him upstairs to see the music and sound gallery, which includes what is claimed to be the world's largest guitar, which you can actually walk inside. There are numerous other opportunities to make music, or noise, depending on your skills, but younger children will be more interested in the huge range of challenging puzzles and games next door. Here we found lots of puzzles of the 'move all the pieces until they go from smallest to largest' and 'move the tangled rope from top to bottom' type, the

sort where there's always a bit of a catch and you need to concentrate very hard. There were plenty of grown-ups hiding from their children trying to get enough time to themselves to solve their chosen puzzle. We intrigued ourselves as we built a bridge that was strong enough for us all to trit-trot across but which had no nails, no screws, no glue, no nothing to hold it together. And don't forget to sit in the chair which spins faster and faster as you hold gyroscopes of different sizes. Great fun, but what is it all about?

The beauty of a place like this is that everyone enjoys something different about it. You can learn all about electricity, sound and lasers, and get that special 'hands on' understanding of why things do what they do, and why sometimes the world is even more extraordinary than you ever imagined. Older children are well catered-for with live science shows every Sunday afternoon, and hourly talks on the stars at weekends and school holidays in the crawl-in Stardome (under-fives not admitted). For younger children too, it's all very immediate, and it took three more attempts at the bubble machine before our son rediscovered his earlier determination to see what the shop had to offer. . .

Fact File

- ADDRESS: The Exploratory Hands-on Science Centre, Bristol Old Station, Temple Meads, Bristol, Avon
- TELEPHONE: 0117 907 5000
- DIRECTIONS: Follow brown tourist signs from city centre
- PUBLIC TRANSPORT: Train to Bristol Temple Meads Station
- DISTANCE: In city centre
- TRAVEL TIME: 15 minutes
- OPENING: Daily 10.00am-5.00pm
- PRICES: Adults £5.00, children £3.50, family £15.00, under-5's free
- RESTAURANT FACILITIES: Yes, at weekends
- NAPPY CHANGING FACILITIES: Yes
- HIGH CHAIRS: Yes
- DOGS: No
- PUSHCHAIR-FRIENDLY: Yes
- NEARBY: Georgian House 0117 921 1362

The National Birds of Prey Centre

"The Eagle has Landed . . ."

THIS IS ONE OF THOSE PLACES WHERE YOU'LL SEE SOMETHING THAT you thought you knew about from watching television or films and discover that there really is nothing like the real thing!

The first thing to bear in mind is that you need to time your visit so as not to miss the flying displays because these are what make the Birds of Prey Centre a unique and quite wonderful experience. Once you've felt the air move on your face as an owl swooshes past you and seen eagles fly, you know that any wildlife programme, however good, is still only television.

Because we'd cut it a bit fine we went straight to the flying field when we arrived – having visited the centre before, we knew that we'd get a lot more than just the impressive sight of magnificent birds in flight – the humans too put on a great show. John, in particular seems to be a born comic, as is Jemima Parry-Jones, the owner of the centre. The birds are

"You'll recognise the African white-backed vultures from Jungle Book"

flown every day; only heavy rain, strong winds or fog will keep them grounded. Some fly more energetically than others: the eagles have apparently learnt that they don't need to do much to get food so they do the bare minimum. And the American black vultures we saw flying are apparently much happier walking; though we were fortunate enough to be there to see all four take to the skies together for the first time – something the handlers had been working towards throughout the season. The four we saw were called Moet, Chandon, Dom and Perignon – each year the new birds born at the centre are named according to the year's chosen theme, and that

year it was alcohol! With two of them on the lawn in front of the house and two on the flying field they flew back and forth, responding to calls (and food), gliding silently and hugely across the space in front of us. After the vultures, the lanner falcon came on. Although I've seen birds of prey hovering high above the fields where we live, I've never seen one 'stoop' – diving with folded wings at huge speed from a great height to catch their prey and it's a thrilling sight.

The highlight of a visit here may well be the flying itself but there's lots more to see: a hawk walk where the flying birds are tethered when they're not in the air; the owl courtyard (there's something quite special about the look you get from an owl); and whatever you do, don't miss the huge aviaries housing birds with reputations as big as themselves – the African white-backed vultures (you'll recognise them from *Jungle Book*), golden eagles and, my favourite, the Andean condor. Until you've seen one of these it's impossible to believe a bird could be this size; the tail feathers look like oars for a small dinghy.

Before setting off for home and to prepare ourselves for the gift shop (just how little could we get away with today?) we were persuaded to stop off at the adventure play area for 10 minutes in exchange for a coffee-shop stop. There are lots of picnic benches nearby so you could spend a whole day here.

A final piece of advice is to buy the guide book, written by Jemima Parry-Jones: it's informative, nicely presented . . . and it made me laugh out loud.

Fact File

● ADDRESS: The National Birds of Prey Centre, Newent, Gloucestershire
● TELEPHONE: 01531 820286
● DIRECTIONS: M5, junction 11 to Newent, A40 to Highnam. Follow signs to Newent then brown tourist signs
● PUBLIC TRANSPORT: No
● DISTANCE: 38 miles
● TRAVEL TIME: 1 hour
● OPENING: Daily from February 1 to November 30, 10.30am-5.30pm (dusk if earlier)
● PRICES: £4.95 adults, £2.90 children, under-4's free, family ticket £14.50
● RESTAURANT FACILITIES: Yes
● NAPPY CHANGING FACILITIES: No
● HIGH CHAIRS: Yes
● DOGS: No
● PUSHCHAIR-FRIENDLY: Yes
● NEARBY: Three Choirs Vineyard (01531 890223)

Rode Bird Gardens

ARRIVING AT RODE BIRD GARDENS, WE FELT WE'D SLIPPED BACK IN time about 30 years. There is nothing modern or up-to-the minute about its entrance, shop or cafeteria and it feels as if little has changed since the old Manor house in Rode first became an all-bird zoo. Buy yourselves a guide book and the first thing you'll read is a piece of advice: 'take your time – you will see a lot more'. Taking that advice and the pair of binoculars we'd remembered to bring certainly ensured that we thoroughly enjoyed our visit.

It's not until you visit a place like this that you have your eyes opened to the real beauty of birds – it's all very well to have seen vibrantly coloured macaws and parrots on the television, but to have three slice through the air above your head in a blaze of colour is magical, the sort of experience that makes you laugh out loud with pleasure. How on earth . . ? we wondered and the guide book told us: that it takes almost a year to train a macaw to fly free and return to its aviary, but, yes, they do sometimes go missing and have to be retrieved.

"The cockatoo with his feathers all puffed up, looking like George III with his extravagantly curled and powdered wig!"

We wandered slowly down towards the lake and ponds where we discovered cranes in plumage so elegant they looked as if they'd just walked off a catwalk. Our tour soon found us at Woodland Central Station, the starting point for a scenic half-mile journey through the woodland and across the lawns of Rode. The birds are by now so used to the train that they apparently sometimes stand on the line and refuse to move – at least that's one problem British Rail never had to report! Going late in the season and out of school holidays we didn't have to queue for the train but in the height of the season you may have to wait 10 minutes or so. It costs an extra £1.10 per adult and 90p for children. One 10-minute journey wasn't enough for our four-year-old however, so he and I stayed on the train and did the trip a second time while my husband sat happily on a bench in the sunshine with the baby on his knee and a variety of pheasants ambling about by his feet.

We caught sight of Pets' Corner from the train but decided that the winged and wonderful birds in the main gardens were more interesting so didn't give it a closer look. There are some wonderful things to see at Rode, but the two birds that stuck in our memories, and that

☞ you really must make sure you go and see, were the Secretary Bird with its astonishingly arrogant walk – alarmingly large and somewhat frightening when you realise that it's a bird of prey. It's called the Secretary Bird because of the way the black feathers on the back of its neck resemble the quill pens used by secretaries in the days before Biros and word processors. And then there's the cockatoo with his feathers all puffed up and out, looking like George III with his extravagantly curled and powdered wig! Having rashly mentioned that people keep budgies and parrots as pets we had a challenging journey home, trying to explain why we wouldn't be getting one of them to sit in the corner of our living room!

There are several special events planned here in 1999, such as steam rallies and an egg hunt. Telephone for more details.

Fact File

- ADDRESS: The Rode Bird Gardens, Rode, near Bath, Somerset
- TELEPHONE: 01373 830326
- DIRECTIONS: A36 from Bath, turn off at Red Lion, Woolverton and follow brown signs
- PUBLIC TRANSPORT: Bus service from Bath to Woolverton (half a mile from gardens)
- DISTANCE: 30 miles
- TRAVEL TIME: 40 minutes
- OPENING: Daily 10.00am-6.00pm (summer), to dusk in winter
- PRICES: Adults £5.00, children £2.50, family £14.50, under-3's free
- RESTAURANT FACILITIES: Yes (summer)
- NAPPY CHANGING FACILITIES: Yes
- HIGH CHAIRS: Yes
- DOGS: No
- PUSHCHAIR-FRIENDLY: Yes
- NEARBY: Iford Manor Gardens (01225 863146), Woodland Park & Smokey Oak Railway (01373 822238)

Slimbridge Wildfowl & Wetland Centre

A VISIT TO THE WILDFOWL AND WETLANDS TRUST AT SLIMBRIDGE takes the time-honoured treat of feeding the ducks onto an altogether different plane. The Trust estimates that there are some 8,000 wildfowl here, enough to keep the most ardent bird-spotter busy.

For us, Slimbridge was a triumph. We set out in what seemed to be quite promising weather, but by the time we arrived the heavens had opened and cats and dogs were pouring down on us, and the prospect of a rain-sodden walk around the vast area that is Slimbridge wasn't appealing – the fact was, it was nice weather for ducks. Undeterred, we had our picnic in the car, put the baby in the backpack, the three-year-old in his coat, the umbrella up and off we went. And we were so pleased that the weather hadn't put us off. Armed with 30p's worth of duck food which was carefully decanted into my son's pockets we set off to feed the ducks. And who'd have guessed there were so many with blue beaks?

> **"There are rain shelters at strategic intervals along the Walkabout Route"**

Or that flamingos, beautiful as they are, are also very smelly! Slimbridge, in fact, is home to all six of the world's flamingo varieties – most of them from South America. We were lucky enough, too, to see a pair of magnificent black swans with their five cygnets.

On a rain-drenched day like the one we'd chosen for our visit, we were pleased to find that there are rain shelters at strategic intervals along the Walkabout Route, which leads you on a walk about a mile long through the various pens – including the North American pen, the African, European and Australian pens – past all the flamingos and to Swan Lake. Then there are paths which take you away from the main route to the hides, and

don't miss the Tropical House, a dramatic change of scene, especially on the day we went, as you enter a mini-tropical rainforest, following a jungle stream to a pool at the bottom of a waterfall. You'll need to keep your eyes open to spot the birds living in here, but take a few minutes to sit quietly and you'll soon see hummingbirds.

When we'd finished our walk we were diverted from a much-needed cup of tea by the lure of PondZone, a lottery-funded addition to Slimbridge, where we did a quick bit of pond-dipping to see what we could find. The diversity of life that appears from underneath the surface of a pond is amazing, and you can then look at what's been found under a microscope.

If you're looking for something to make you think, the Zarg and Zora H_2O trail boards are a mine of information about water and how we can save it. Slightly older children can pick up a question sheet to take with them, then at the end they can take their completed sheet to the Operation H_2O Computer to check their answers – fun and educational! During the school holidays look out for a number of bird-themed activities for children: generally quizzes, special trails or crafts are available.

We ended our visit feeling surprisingly dry, with a warm glow that came from having had such a good time in spite of the miserable weather. Try it yourselves!

Fact File

- ADDRESS: Wildfowl & Wetlands Trust, Slimbridge, Gloucestershire
- TELEPHONE: 01453 890333
- DIRECTIONS: M5 junctions 13 and 14, follow brown signs
- PUBLIC TRANSPORT: Cam & Dursley train station (01452 529501), then a short journey by bicycle or taxi; by bus contact the Public Transport Enquiry Line (01452 425543) for a timetable
- DISTANCE: 25 miles
- TRAVEL TIME: 40 minutes
- OPENING: Daily 9.30am-5.30pm (5.00pm in winter)
- PRICES: Adults £5.25, children £3.00, under-4's free
- RESTAURANT FACILITIES: Yes
- NAPPY CHANGING FACILITIES: Yes
- HIGH CHAIRS: Yes
- DOGS: No
- PUSHCHAIR-FRIENDLY: Yes
- NEARBY: Berkeley Castle (01453 810332)

SS Great Britain & Maritime Heritage Centre

"Yo Ho Ho and a Bottle of Rum!"

THE SS GREAT BRITAIN HAS A UNIQUE PLACE IN THE HISTORY OF maritime transport, being the first ocean-going propeller-driven iron ship and designed by Isambard Kingdom Brunel. After a varied career she was ignominiously abandoned in 1886 in the Falklands, but in 1970 she was rescued and brought back, a tired and rusting relic, to be restored in the very place where she started her long (a total of 1.25 million sea miles) career.

She lies in Great Western Dock where work goes on to restore her to her former glory. Walking out onto the dockside and looking up at her she's certainly an imposing sight. We had to leave the buggy in the shop which meant carrying the baby, not ideal as there are several narrow flights of stairs between decks, so a sling or backpack is advisable if you've got a baby or an I-don't want-to-walk toddler.

"Up on the top deck not one of us could resist taking a turn at the wheel"

Up on the top deck not one of us could resist taking a turn at the wheel and imagining ourselves in charge of this magnificent ship as it pitched and tossed across the high seas – our four-year-old was well acquainted with the principle of this kind of ship from watching a *Barney the Dinosaur* video and he thought he could sail all the way to Imagination Island!

If you start at the top as we did, your next move will be down the stairs to the deck where the cabins would have been. Here you'll find a cabin that's been restored to its original splendour but, in fact it's so small it's hard to believe it was first class – there was barely room to turn around in it. A notice close by told us that Charles Dickens had crossed the Atlantic in an identical cabin, apparently the crossing took 14 days. But she only made the journey to America four times because gold was discovered in Australia and that was where people wanted to go. The SS Great Britain made the 60-day trip 32 times in all, and we wondered how many people who made the gold digger's trip made a fortune!

If you can, have a quick peep at the fully restored and refurbished dining saloon – a beautiful room, all marble pillars and mirrors. We were almost immediately shooed out as there was a lunch going on, but we got enough of a look for our son to be fascinated at the idea of a boat having such an elaborate room. Actually, he was amazed at it having rooms at all, as his experience of boats had until now been limited to boats in the bath or, slightly larger, on boating ponds with Daddy at the oars.

☞   Docked alonside the SS Great Britain is a modern-day replica of a 15th century merchant ship, "The Matthew", which in 1997 did a repeat run of the original's voyage to Newfoundland in 1497. You can visit her upper decks and play around with the tiller and the riggings. Having finished with the boats wander around to the other side of the dock, where we discovered the Bristol Blue glass works. Our son stood transfixed watching the glass blowers at work and I dredged my memory for what I knew of glass manufacture. Children don't let you off easily and the sight of glass in its liquid form needed explanation!

Don't be tempted to skip the Maritime Heritage Centre, a small but brilliantly presented museum which reveals the history of ship-building in Bristol from the earliest days. We loved the life-sized models of men at work on the SS Great Britain and all the sounds of ship-building that echoed through the museum. Our son couldn't get enough of pressing the button to start the welder welding and watching the sparks fly. Happily he wasn't welded to the spot and we managed to prise him away in the end.

Fact File

● ADDRESS: SS Great Britain & Maritime Heritage Centre, Great Western Dock, Gas Ferry Road, Bristol, Avon
● TELEPHONE: 0117 926 0680
● DIRECTIONS: Follow signs from Bristol city centre
● PUBLIC TRANSPORT: Bus and ferry
● DISTANCE: 2 miles
● TRAVEL TIME: 10 minutes
● OPENING: Daily 10.00am-5.30pm (1 April to 31 October) or to 4.30pm the rest of the year
● PRICES: Adults £6.00, children £3.50, family £16.00, under-5's free
● RESTAURANT FACILITIES: Small tearoom
● NAPPY CHANGING FACILITIES: No
● HIGH CHAIRS: No
● DOGS: No
● PUSHCHAIR-FRIENDLY: No
● NEARBY: Clifton Suspension Bridge, Observatory and Caves (0117 974 1212); City Museum and Art Gallery (0117 922 3571)

Techniquest

THE FIRST THING OUR FOUR-YEAR-OLD DID AS WE WALKED INTO
Techniquest was to grab hold of the beach ball that he
discovered floating in mid-air in front of him. And if you
watch for a little while, you'll see that no-one, big or
small, can resist doing the same. The why of it is
irrelevant, what matters is the excitement of something
completely new and unexpected. And this is what makes
Techniquest so special. *At Techniquest no-one says
"Don't Touch"* is one of their selling lines, and it's
perfectly true. In fact to get the best out of your visit,
children – and parents – need to touch, feel, press, look,
jump, pull, shout, whisper, all the time.

Young ones will just enjoy the experience because
everything is a new toy. Our son was fascinated by Orbit,
a model which used balls to demonstrate the movement
of the planets but only because he could throw them in
at the top and catch them
when they came out at
the side. He's saving
himself for how the sun
moves round the earth.
Older ones may well ask
taxing questions that need
a decent answer,
"Mummy, why does the
boat sink in the
bubbles?", and if your
grasp of science means

> ## "To get the best out of your visit just touch, feel, press, look, jump, pull, shout, and whisper, all the time"

you can't even understand the explanation that's
provided, in English and Welsh, help is at hand. Just ask
one of the many attendants and you'll find someone
who's ready and able to give you the simple answers you
need – or more detailed ones if your child refuses to be
fobbed off as easily as you!

It is almost unfair on Techniquest to single out
particular exhibits from the 160 on display. Our son loved
the Ames Room, where all the walls and furnishings were
peculiarly shaped and sized to demonstrate the effects of

perspective – you have to be there! He also revelled in all the water exhibits, but best of all was the corner where we could jump with arms spread wide and legs kicking the air to leave our shadows in colour on the wall. This had the three of us giggling insanely until embarrassment got the better of our four-year-old and he decided we should see something else.

The great thing about coming here is that parents will have their own favourites too, but sadly for them they're never the same as their children's. I was just about to solve one particular puzzle when I was dragged away. This makes Techniquest sheer torture for adults who know that just another 30 seconds and they'd have the answer . . . children aren't keen on the sitting down and solving, they love the doing, watching and making things. You'll be lucky if you escape with only one visit to the mirror maze and seeing yourself on television is endlessly appealing! There's also a Planetarium with regular 45-minute shows throughout the day, but it's not recommended for under-sixes. However there are 30-minute interactive demonstrations in the Science Theatre at weekends and school holidays which are designed for all ages.

If you can prise your kids away from all there is to see and do, touch and move, and you've got any time left, you'll find it well worthwhile to have an explore around Cardiff Bay. After Techniquest, The Welsh Industrial and Maritime Museum seems very traditional (lots of Don't Touch notices), but outside, joy of joys, is a real (static) steam engine where children can climb into the driver's cab and just pretend. We took turns doing this while the other nipped off to browse round the craft centre – do try and do this as it's packed full of beautiful things.

Techniquest is a real 'something for everyone' day out, and provides food for thought for some time to come as we discovered in the car on the way home when a thoughtful voice said, "Mummy, when I pressed the button, why did that balloon go up to the ceiling?"

Fact File

- ADDRESS: Techniquest, Stuart Street, Cardiff
- TELEPHONE: 01222 475475
- DIRECTIONS: M4 to junction 33, follow brown tourist signs for Cardiff Bay
- PUBLIC TRANSPORT: No.8 bus from Cardiff Wood Street to Cardiff Bay
- DISTANCE: 60 miles
- TRAVEL TIME: 1 hour 15 minutes
- OPENING: Daily 9.30am-4.30pm (weekdays), 10.30am-5.00pm (weekends and bank holidays)
- PRICES: Adults £5.00, children £3.75, family £14.50, under-5's free
- RESTAURANT FACILITIES: Yes
- NAPPY-CHANGING FACILITIES: Yes
- HIGH CHAIRS: Yes
- DOGS: No
- PUSHCHAIR-FRIENDLY: Yes
- NEARBY: Cardiff Castle (01222 878100), Welsh Industrial & Maritime Museum (01222 481919)

The Great Outdoors

Barrington Court Gardens

THIS BEAUTIFUL HOUSE WITH ITS STUNNING GARDENS HAS A VERY special place in National Trust history, being the first house in the country to be given to them. Soon afterwards it was let to one Colonel Arthur Lyle who set about restoring the beautiful, but sadly run-down, sixteenth century house. Presently the house is closed, but, as the interiors of grand properties are never the most relaxing of places when you're accompanied by small children, it's the gardens which, for families, are the real attraction of a visit to Barrington Court. With the children sufficiently diverted by the grassy lawns and hide-and-seek hedges, you'll also find much here to delight and inspire every scale of gardener – from a weekend potterer to a never-out-of-the-garden fanatic.

> **"The walled Kitchen Garden proved to be the biggest hit of the day"**

We had a map of the estate and followed the recommended route through a seemingly endless avenue of horse chestnut tree 'houses' where the children collected armfuls, then pocketfuls and finally, handbagfuls of conkers. The original plans for the formal gardens were designed by Gertrude Jekyll, although they apparently had to be modified a little as they were executed, and the children were fascinated when we explained that the idea was to have three separate 'rooms', decorated in different colours.

We were most impressed with the Lily Garden which

had the brightest colours – fiery orange blooms merging into scarlet and crimson before fading away to pale pink, yellow and white, creating an altogether amazing effect. Once the children had discovered they couldn't pick the flowers they lost interest in them and left us to marvel at the planting while they scurried in and out of the paths. In the Rose and Iris Garden the soft pastel themes of pink and purple failed to make a big impression on the children though the sundial caught their attention and provoked a confusing discussion about how we tell the time!

The walled Kitchen Garden proved to be the biggest hit of the day. This really feels like a room and the children loved the fruit trees trained across the walls

and the pool marking the centre of the garden. It even has a scarecrow to pull faces at. We adults stood looking around us at the Ham stone walls and felt that time had stood still but the children found it hard to believe that, once upon a time, all the fruit and vegetables the family needed would have been grown in here. But they were adamant that we should buy some of the home-grown vegetables on sale to take home for their tea. (One way to ensure they eat their greens!)

All the talk about days gone by hadn't diverted them from the very modern carton of juice they wanted after all their exertions and, after a quick drink stop, we piled back into the car and headed homewards. Perhaps I could get a bit of weeding done before bedtime . . .

Fact File

- ADDRESS: Barrington Court, Barrington, near Ilminster, Somerset
- TELEPHONE: 01460 241938
- DIRECTIONS: M5 to junction 25, A358 to Thronfalcon traffic lights, left on A378 to Curry Rivel, then follow brown tourist signs
- PUBLIC TRANSPORT: No
- DISTANCE: 50 miles
- TRAVEL TIME: 1 hour 10 minutes
- OPENING: 20 March to 31 October, daily except Fridays, 11.00am-5.30pm (last admission 5.00pm)
- PRICES: Adults £4.00, children £2.00. Free to National Trust members
- RESTAURANT FACILITIES: Yes
- NAPPY CHANGING FACILITIES: No
- HIGH CHAIRS: Yes
- DOGS: No
- PUSHCHAIR-FRIENDLY: Yes (gardens and cafe only)
- NEARBY: National Trust's Montacute House (01935 823289)

Bowood House

BOWOOD HOUSE IS A GREAT EXAMPLE OF HOW TO MARRY THE attractions (to adults) of a stately home with beautifully manicured gardens and extensive grounds with the need (of children) to burn off a great deal of energy and play till they drop. For Bowood has an adventure playground that will keep the kids active until they simply can't slide down another slide, climb any more stairs to any more crows' nests or sail another mile on the brilliant pirates' ship.

The playground has been designed to make the best possible use of the trees and hanging walkways connect the many pieces of equipment. You need to be ready to catch a lightweight child at the bottom of the slides as they're longer than any I've ever seen and give a small child time to build up a considerable speed. We started at the playground and for at least an hour it looked as though we wouldn't be going anywhere else. Unsurprisingly, it was only hunger that finally extracted our son from the pirates' galleon – that and a bit of adventurous clambering up the cargo nets by Mummy to retrieve him! The playground does get busy so you'll need to keep your eyes peeled with small ones.

> **"An adventure playground that will keep the kids active for hours"**

When you finally drag them away, head along the side of the Capability Brown lake and up towards the Cascade and the Hermit's Cave. It's about a 10-minute walk and the gloom of the 'real' cave, complete with fossils and precious stones on the walls should impress most children. That and the stories you could tell about living as a hermit in a cave! The Cascade itself is 25 ft of marvellous crashing and splashing water – great on a hot day. Call in at the Doric Temple to admire the view across the lake before heading back.

The rest of the grounds are extensive and ideal for romping around. You can choose open grassy and tree-

dotted
parkland,
resplendent with daffodils in
spring, or the more formal terraces with steps,
walls and gravel paths around the house. The
rhodedendrons are magnificent in season, and, if you like
that sort of thing, there is a guided walk you can do
around the most impressive (£3.00 adults, children free).
You can picnic almost anywhere and most of the paths
are good for buggies.

   If you can, steal a look round the house with or
without the children it's well worth it. The Orangery
houses an exhibition detailing the history of the house
and gardens, whilst other rooms that are open are the
laboratory where Dr Joseph Priestley discovered oxygen in
1774, an impressive library and a rather beautiful chapel.
There's a stunning collection of watercolours including
work by JMW Turner and Edward Lear, as well as
Exhibition Galleries where objects belonging to the
Lansdowne family over the past two centuries are
displayed. These include many elaborate and beautiful
pieces collected while the 5th Lord Lansdowne was

Viceroy of India from 1888-1894. "They look like trowels" I overheard another visitor say in disbelief, but on closer inspection they were indeed trowels – ceremonial trowels used in tree-plantings. The jewels in the crown are the stunning collection given to Admiral Viscount Keith at the time of the Napoleonic Wars.

Fact File

- ADDRESS: Bowood House and Gardens, Calne, Wiltshire
- TELEPHONE: 01249 812102
- DIRECTIONS: A420 from Bristol and follow brown tourist signs from Chippenham
- PUBLIC TRANSPORT: X55 bus via Chippenham and Calne, and 10-minute walk from road
- DISTANCE: 15 miles
- TRAVEL TIME: 25 minutes
- OPENING: Daily 11.00am-6.00pm, 27 March to 31 October
- PRICES: Adults £5.50, children £3.20, under-5's free
- RESTAURANT FACILITIES: Yes
- NAPPY-CHANGING FACILITIES: Yes
- HIGH CHAIRS: Yes
- DOGS: No
- PUSHCHAIR-FRIENDLY: Yes
- NEARBY: Sheldon Manor (01249 653120)

Cheddar Gorge

CHEDDAR IS A VERY GOOD DAY OUT WITH LOTS TO DO AND SEE EVEN if it has been fairly heavily commercialised, but it's certainly not a cheap one. It's true that the ticket you buy entitles you to entry to six attractions but if you don't visit them all then that's your hard luck – and £2.50 for parking underneath the sheer cliffs seems, pardon the pun, a bit steep. However, the caves are quite simply extraordinary – the depth, extent and sheer beauty are breathtaking – and are manageable with a buggy almost all the way around.

With four under-fives we limited ourselves to the tour of Gough's Cave, the largest of the illuminated showcaves and a stunning reminder of just how old the earth is, the caverns having been carved out of the rock by the meltwaters of the last Ice Age. This is nature at her most dramatic, creating extraordinary sculptures highlighted by the endlessly seeping water running over and round them. And once you're back in the 20th century and recall what you've just experienced and what lies under your feet it seems somehow even more awe-inspiring.

"This is nature at her most dramatic"

Cox's Cave is home to Crystal Quest, a fantasy adventure. The initial darkness may prove too daunting for younger children, but older ones would love it. It's a sort of adventure quest done in scenes and tableaux with a story theme and commentary that are set off as you pass. All jolly stirring stuff.

Back outside again and blinking in the light, we had a picnic at the foot of Jacob's Ladder – 370 steps that climb to the top of the Gorge and from which you can see Glastonbury Tor. To go up it you'll need a backpack for children who can't walk far. The climb represents the earth's history, so as you climb, boards tell you at intervals what point you've reached and what would have existed then. It's an interesting presentation of the earth's story and one that conveys the incredible length of time before man and civilisation made their appearance. Even when you reach the last step of Jacob's Ladder, the climb isn't quite over. Another 50-odd stairs and you'll be at the top of Pavey's lookout tower – not to be missed as this is the place to get a truly panoramic view of the surrounding countryside and an appreciation of just how deep the gorge is.

If you're feeling energetic and your children are older and out of buggies, which we weren't and they aren't, you can tackle the three-mile clifftop walk which starts from the top of Jacob's Ladder, but allow two hours for it. With so much else to do in Cheddar you'll need to plan your day carefully to fit everything in. For those who like to conserve energy, a 15-minute guided tour on an open-top bus runs throughout the summer months (included in admission price).

☞   It's a strange fact that coming down loads of steps is somehow more difficult than the going up and we reached the bottom of Jacob's Ladder with leg muscles protesting, but not enough to prevent us carrying on down the Gorge to the Cheddar Rural Life Museum where you can see the world-famous Cheddar cheese being made, candles created and wool spun. We were intrigued as we watched a clump of wool being combed out, twisted and fed onto the spinning wheel to be turned into something familiar. Unfortunately the Rural Life Museum isn't part of the all-in ticket and will cost you extra, but even without it you'll find more than enough to keep everyone entertained. Even after our long and tiring day we left with the feeling that we hadn't quite seen it all.

Fact File

- ADDRESS: Cheddar Showcaves and Gorge, Cheddar, Somerset
- TELEPHONE: 01934 742343
- DIRECTIONS: M5 to junction 22, then A371 (A38) and follow brown tourist signs
- PUBLIC TRANSPORT: 126 bus from Wells or Weston-super-mere
- DISTANCE: 30 miles
- TRAVEL TIME: 45 minutes
- OPENING: Daily 10.00am-5.00pm (summer), 10.30am-4.30pm (winter)
- PRICES: Adults £7.50, children £4.00, family £19.00, under-5's free
- RESTAURANT FACILITIES: Yes
- NAPPY CHANGING FACILITIES: Yes
- HIGH CHAIRS: Yes
- DOGS: No
- PUSHCHAIR-FRIENDLY: Mostly (not Jacob's Ladder)
- NEARBY: Cheddar Rural Life Museum (01934 742810)

Dyrham Park

AS WE DROVE DOWN THE LONG AND ELEGANTLY CURVING DRIVE
towards the big house, my husband commented "I can
just see myself being driven home here after a day up in
town". He meant in a coach with a pair of greys pulling it,
sweeping down to the imposing front door to be met by a
footman . . . and he was quite right. Dyrham really does
have the capacity to transport you instantly backwards in
time, though there was a lot that was modern in the
number of cars parked in the car park!

Dyrham is a National Trust property, built for William
Blathwayt, Secretary at War and Secretary of State to
William III between 1691 and 1710 with the rooms little
changed since then, though more recently it was featured
in the film, *The Remains of the Day*. We started our visit
with a tour of the house, always best when you're with
little people. Our four-year-old was very taken with the
massive stone eagle
perched on the roof above
the front door. Inside we
had to surrender the
buggy which was whisked
away into a room behind
a hidden door. This meant
carrying the baby – it's
not ideal but if your child
is walking they'll manage

"Lawns that might have been cut with nail scissors rolling gently down towards the lake"

the tour around the house. It's an undeniable fact that
the main attraction of a visit to a stately home is never
going to be the house itself when you have children with
you, and the tour will always be a bit whistle-stop. It
certainly was for us here.

But outside there is plenty to amuse the whole family.
The house is surrounded by an ancient deer park, but
when we went the deer had all wisely sought somewhere
shady to while away a very hot day. Walk through the
stable yard to the formal gardens which are picture-
postcard immaculate, with the Parish Church sitting
dramatically above them and with lawns that might have

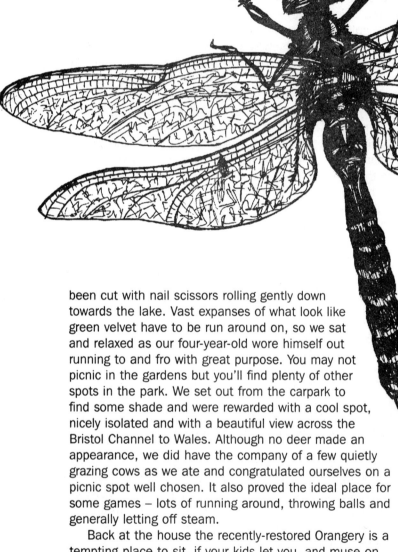

been cut with nail scissors rolling gently down towards the lake. Vast expanses of what look like green velvet have to be run around on, so we sat and relaxed as our four-year-old wore himself out running to and fro with great purpose. You may not picnic in the gardens but you'll find plenty of other spots in the park. We set out from the carpark to find some shade and were rewarded with a cool spot, nicely isolated and with a beautiful view across the Bristol Channel to Wales. Although no deer made an appearance, we did have the company of a few quietly grazing cows as we ate and congratulated ourselves on a picnic spot well chosen. It also proved the ideal place for some games – lots of running around, throwing balls and generally letting off steam.

Back at the house the recently-restored Orangery is a tempting place to sit, if your kids let you, and muse on the view of the gardens, whilst surrounded by oranges in

the summer, or a host of
other plants in the winter
months. If you tell them
that the plants are
brought in out of the cold to
holiday in the sun, maybe
they'll let you have a quick rest in there
too . . !

Fact File

- ADDRESS: Dyrham Park, Dyrham, near Bath, Somerset
- TELEPHONE: 0117 937 2501
- DIRECTIONS: M4 to junction 18, then A46 and follow brown tourist signs
- PUBLIC TRANSPORT: Ryan's bus from stand B1 Dorchester Street, Bath, runs direct to Park at 1.00pm on Fridays and Saturdays, returning at 5.00pm (01225 424157)
- DISTANCE: 12 miles
- TRAVEL TIME: 30 minutes
- OPENING: Daily 27 March to 31 October 11.00am-5.00pm. Park only Wednesdays & Thursdays (from 12noon)
- PRICES: Park & garden adults £2.50, children £1.20. House, park & garden adults £5.50, children £2.70, family £13.50. Free to National Trust members
- RESTAURANT FACILITIES: Yes
- NAPPY CHANGING FACILITIES: Yes
- HIGH CHAIRS: Yes
- DOGS: No (dog walking area provided)
- PUSHCHAIR FRIENDLY: Yes
- NEARBY: The American Museum (01225 460503)

Hestercombe Gardens

*"Mary, Mary, quite contrary,
how does your garden grow?"*

CHOOSE A FINE DAY WITH NO THREAT OF RAIN FOR A VISIT TO
Hestercombe because everything here is outside – except
the tea rooms and the gift shop! But it's one of those
wonderful places that has attractions for everyone: plenty
of space for the children to run around and let off steam
combined with the grown-up appeal of a beautiful garden.

1997 was the first time the gardens had been opened
in 125 years, restoration of them having begun in 1991.
They were originally the creation of Coplestone Warre
Bampfylde, a leading landscape gardener of the 18th
century. And even though the work goes on, what was
unveiled last year was simply stunning: 40 acres of
formal and landscape gardens complete with lakes and
temples, fountains, staircases and
statues. These Georgian landscaped
gardens extend over 35 acres and
offer quite spectacular walks. It's
amazing to realise that these were
designed and built between 1750
and 1786 and that only now are they
being brought back to life.

**"Something
unexpected
around almost
every corner"**

You'll be constantly surprised as you tour the gardens
by discovering something unexpected around almost every
corner. Grab a (free) map at the entrance, as there are
no tours, leaving you at liberty to go at your own pace.
It's best to follow a map though, as there are few
signposts making it easy to get lost along some of the
wooded paths.

The gardens do belong to a house, but Hestercombe
House is now the headquarters of Somerset Fire Brigade
and isn't open to the public. However, the fire engines we
saw parked close to the entrance provided the first thrill

of the day. Then it was off through a delightful wooded area that opened out into a picturesque walk around Pear Pond, which looks like a tadpole with a very long tail on the map! Because we were loaded down with all our picnic paraphernalia we decided on an early lunch. The grounds in front of the beautiful Orangery building make an ideal spot – loads of lawns for the children to run around on without ever disappearing from view, and a large tree above to provide shade.

The Edwardian garden is just beautiful, a formal sunken garden, designed by Sir Edwin Lutyens and planted by Gertrude Jekyll, a gardening dream team. However, with its many water features, you'll need eyes in

☞ the back of your head with very young children here.

The real magic of Hestercombe for a family with children is that you never know what's coming next, but you can be sure it'll be something to enchant – we enjoyed the Witches' Cave, a thatched hut of gnarled and twisted tree branches reputedly used by witches in the 18th century and guaranteed to send a shiver or two down the spine! The Great Cascade Waterfall was the biggest surprise of all and thrilled our kids to bits. The adults were quite impressed too, especially when they discovered that the waterfall has been reclaimed from the undergrowth and years of neglect. There is a continuing programme of development, so there will be new things on offer every year. In 1999 look out for the new Alcove seat which will have lovely views.

Heading back to the car park we passed the tea shop and couldn't resist popping in for cups of tea, slices of home-made cake and a really friendly welcome. The gift shop proved equally unmissable and a great source of presents for any gardening-mad relatives or friends. Fresh air, beautiful surroundings and that all-important cup of tea – gardener or not, Hestercombe is utterly irresistible.

Fact File

- ADDRESS: Hestercombe Gardens, Cheddon Fitzpaine, Taunton, Somerset
- TELEPHONE: 01823 413923
- DIRECTIONS: M5 to junction 25 to Taunton, turn right at Great Mills roundabout, then follow signs to Hestercombe
- PUBLIC TRANSPORT: No
- DISTANCE: 45 miles
- TRAVEL TIME: 1 hour 15 minutes
- OPENING: Daily 10.00am-5.00pm
- PRICES: Adults £3.50, children £1.00, under-5's free
- RESTAURANT FACILITIES: Yes
- NAPPY CHANGING FACILITIES: Yes
- HIGH CHAIRS: Yes
- DOGS: Yes
- PUSHCHAIR-FRIENDLY: Limited
- NEARBY: Sheppy's Cider Farm Centre, Taunton (01823 461233)

Jubilee Maze

Amazing – we had no idea that there could be a place that would entertain eight children safely for hours on end but here it is – the Jubilee Maze at Symonds Yat. We bought our tickets and approached the entrance to the maze, where we were greeted by Lindsay Heyes, one of the two brothers who built the maze in 1977 to celebrate the Queen's Silver Jubilee. Dressed for an afternoon's boating at Henley complete with striped blazer, bow tie and boater and holding a brass megaphone, the children were transfixed by him. He treated us to a short history of mazes and an explanation of how they came to design and build the maze here and then the children were off like greyhounds out of the traps.

We had thought that we'd first visit the maze and then head off up towards Yat Rock to find a picnic spot, but it was hard to beat the picnic area beside the maze so we unloaded rugs and cool boxes and settled ourselves around a picnic table ready for the children to refuel when they'd finished racing around the maze. And that's the beauty of this place – they would have been in and out, round

"The kids would have been in and out, round and round, up and down all day if we'd let them"

and round, up and down to the viewing platform all day if we'd let them. There was no restriction on them coming out and going back in and they all became addicted to haring around the circular paths between hedges too high for them to see over, shouting to each other and to their parents as they went.

On the other side of the maze from the picnic area you'll find the Museum of Mazes, which is a good place to pop in to exploit everyone's new enthusiasm for mazes. Here you can trace mazes with your fingers, build them and draw them yourselves in sand. Also on the site and new last year is the Splendour of the Orient; an

Oriental garden, tearoom and shop alongside the Maze. Whilst if you fancy a short riverside stroll you can follow the lane down to the banks of the Wye and on to the beautiful riverside St Dubricius church.

If you're feeling more adventurous and want to make the most of your day, you'll be richly rewarded by a visit to Yat Rock. You can either walk to it downstream from the riverside church, or take a short drive. A climb from the car park takes you to a viewpoint

high above the Wye. From here you'll get the most breathtaking views of the river as it bends its way dramatically through the wooded countryside. If you're visiting the Wye Valley it seems a crime to miss this view and if you're lucky you may also catch a glimpse of the peregrine falcons on the sheer cliffs opposite. Often there'll be a birdwatcher with a telescope trained on the cliffs – ask nicely and he'll let you have a look, too. And if you haven't seen enough you could always drop down to Symonds Yat East and take a short boat trip up the river to the rapids and see the rock from below. We all enjoyed watching the canoeists struggling against the rapids, willing them to find the strength to beat them, only to start all over again! There is so much to do and see at Symonds Yat that the old cliche about it being two days out is really true, but if you pack it all in you'll certainly go home tired but happy after a great day out.

Fact File

- ADDRESS: Jubilee Maze, Symonds Yat West, Ross-on-Wye, Herefordshire
- TELEPHONE: 01600 890360
- DIRECTIONS: M4/M48 over old Severn Bridge, A466 to Monmouth, A40 to Symonds Yat, then follow brown tourist signs
- PUBLIC TRANSPORT: No
- DISTANCE: 45 miles
- TRAVEL TIME: 1 hour
- OPENING: Daily, April to end of October 11.00am-5.00pm. Weekends in March and October, plus February and autumn half term holidays
- PRICES: Adults £3.50, children £2.00, family £9.00, under-5's free
- RESTAURANT FACILITIES: Yes
- NAPPY CHANGING FACILITIES: Yes
- HIGH CHAIRS: Yes
- DOGS: No
- PUSHCHAIR-FRIENDLY: Yes
- NEARBY: Goodrich Castle, Ross-on-Wye (01600 890538)

Westonbirt Arboretum

IT WAS A PERFECT SUNDAY MORNING AT THE END OF OCTOBER, bright sunshine in cloudless blue skies, when we visited Westonbirt. Almost the first thing our son asked as we set off on the Autumn trail was, "Is there a playground here?". There isn't, but it didn't take long – just as long as it took to find the first hiding place tucked inside a clutch of bamboo trees – for him to forget entirely that he'd ever wanted one. The trees themselves provide a perfect playground and huge rhododendron bushes bear witness to long use as hiding places for children who've visited Westonbirt. There are giant trees with trunks so massive that a posse of small children could have hidden undiscovered behind them and trees that have grown in such magical ways that they look as if they've been sculpted. A tree with one of its roots growing back up towards its trunk created a doorway to walk through and back, through and back, through and back and offered as much entertainment as any slide or climbing frame. And we all nearly fell flat on our backs straining to spot the point where a majestic Douglas fir met the sky.

Although the leaflet suggests that the

"Giant trees with trunks so massive that a posse of small children could have hidden undiscovered behind them!"

Arboretum is beautiful in every season, it is impossible to believe that it can ever be more glorious than it is as the acers change clothes for the autumn and emerge dressed in every shade from brightest yellow to the most vivid reds and purples. We'd been tipped off that Acer Glade was spectacular so that was where we headed first. It was a good tip, as entering the glade was a bit like walking into an art gallery, with people standing back just to admire the trees. It had also attracted several photographers with all the equipment – zoom lenses and tripods – preparing to capture nature at her most flamboyant. It certainly brought home the fact that at moments like this art can never better nature.

The walks are not difficult and are nicely manageable with a buggy – with 17 miles of trails you'll only be limited by your stamina. Apart from the Autumn trail you can get leaflets for

a Treasure trail in the Silk Wood (lots of searching for items along the way), and in the Old Arboretum a Great Bear Hunt, aimed at younger children, and two quiz-type trails. Little legs and a pressing need for a loo stop limited us to the Autumn trail after which we returned to the Courtyard Cafe for cups of tea, cans of Coke and some very moreish coffee cake. An unmissable element in

☞ every day out in our family is a visit to the gift shop and this is a particularly good one. It's big, imaginatively stocked and well presented, which means parting with more cash, of course!

On the day we went, and October is their busiest time of year with an additional refreshment marquee, loads of portaloos and parking for thousands of cars laid on, the Arboretum was full of people but the efficiency with which everything was run was extremely impressive and made the busyness irrelevant. Visiting Westonbirt in the autumn also proved to be the springboard for several more hours of entertainment – we collected a bag of fallen leaves in every shape and colour we could find and took them home to create our own autumn pictures: leaf prints littered the house for weeks afterwards!

And although I suspect autumn can't be improved on, we'll certainly be going back in every season because Westonbirt is simply magical and proves that kids don't need to be spoon-fed with playgrounds and entertainments. In a place like this they make their own fun and there's loads of it to be had.

Fact File

- ADDRESS: Westonbirt Arboretum, Tetbury, Gloucestershire
- TELEPHONE: 01666 880220
- DIRECTION: M4 junction 18, then A46 northbound, and A433 to Westonbirt
- PUBLIC TRANSPORT: None
- DISTANCE: 35 miles
- TRAVEL TIME: 30-40 minutes
- OPENING: Daily 10.00am-8.00pm (or dusk if earlier)
- PRICES: Adults £3.80, children £1.00, under-5's free
- RESTAURANT FACILITIES: Yes
- NAPPY CHANGING FACILITIES: Yes
- HIGH CHAIRS: Yes
- DOGS: Yes, except Old Arboretum
- PUSHCHAIR-FRIENDLY: Yes
- NEARBY: Sheldon Manor (01249 653120)

Somewhat Historical

Chepstow Castle & Museum

"This castle hath a pleasant seat . . ."

"I REALLY LIKE CASTLES", SAID OUR FOUR-YEAR-OLD WHEN WE announced we were going to visit Chepstow Castle. "You can do whatever you want", by which he means that he can run around to his heart's content, clamber over old stones, look through arrow slits in impenetrable stone walls and give impromptu performances of nursery rhymes on bits of wall that seem to have evolved quite naturally into stages. We're huge fans of many of the border castles, but Chepstow stands head and shoulders above them all. From its imposing setting on a cliff

"The gently sloping grass of the lower bailey begs to be rolled on"

above the River Severn to its status as the oldest stone-built castle in Britain (the earliest parts of the castle date from 1067), everything about Chepstow seems to be so perfectly castle-ish.

Once through the shop-cum-entrance, with the promise of a soldier to be bought later, we were up the steps and out into the castle itself. The baby sat serenely in her buggy taking it all in but our four-year-old was beside himself with the possibilities. We wanted to go and take a look at the exhibition charting the history of the castle, but instead we were persuaded into Marten's Tower. Round and round and up and up the stone spiral staircase we went, stopping at every 'floor' to take a look

☞

down until we reached the top and then looked up at the ornamental figures adorning the parapet. Down again and before we visited the exhibition we played chase on the gently sloping grass of the lower bailey which begs to be rolled on.

The exhibition has a series of lifesized models of the men who built Chepstow; William fitz Osbern, friend of William the Conqueror, came first followed by the Marshal family 150 years later who extended the castle considerably: all thrilling stuff for soldier-mad kids.

Upstairs is the 'Castle at War' part of the exhibition. Be warned – your arrival will trigger a soundtrack to the re-creation (life-sized again) of a Civil War battle scene. Taking your life in your hands you walk between the opposing sides! There's an invitation too, to try on a trooper's and a pikeman's helmets to see how you'd have looked. They were so heavy it's a wonder they didn't all knock themselves out before they ever saw a battlefield. We got as far as the Great Tower, the oldest part of the castle which once stood three storeys tall, but couldn't go any further because there were men at work. We asked what the man in the yellow jacket was doing abseiling down the cliff and discovered that in the course of last year the cliff had been bolted back together to prevent the castle falling into the river.

Back in the car park, we stopped briefly to dump the picnic stuff in the car and headed across the road to Chepstow's small but perfectly formed museum – it's well worth a visit and makes an ideal introduction to the concept of museums for the under-fives. They've even taken the trouble to produce a sheet with pictures of exhibits for them to try and find. Our four-year-old needed a little help but had great fun looking and it provided a great focus for the visit.

Our advice to anyone planning a day out in Chepstow is to leave plenty of time to sample the teashops and take a look at the town as well as the castle. Sadly we only discovered this when we ran out of time . . .

Fact File

- ADDRESS: Chepstow Castle, Chepstow, Monmouthshire
- TELEPHONE: 01291 624065
- DIRECTIONS: M4 to M48 junction, across Old Severn Bridge, follow signs for Chepstow
- PUBLIC TRANSPORT: British Rail to Chepstow and 30-minute walk
- DISTANCE: 15 miles
- TRAVEL TIME: 30 minutes
- OPENING: Daily 9.30am-5.00pm from 29 March to 31 October; 9.30am-4.00pm Monday to Saturday and 11.00am-4.00pm Sundays from 1 November to end March
- PRICES: Adults £3.00, children £2.00, family £8.00, under-5's free
- RESTAURANT FACILITIES: No
- NAPPY CHANGING FACILITIES: Yes (car park)
- HIGH CHAIRS: No
- DOGS: No
- PUSHCHAIR-FRIENDLY: Yes
- NEARBY: Chepstow Museum (01291 625981)

Clearwell Caves and Puzzle Wood

"I WANT TO GO IN THE BUGGY BECAUSE IT'S CAVES," CAME THE plaintive cry from my four-year-old. So it was that I found myself, single-handed, with a baby on my back, manhandling a buggy around the extensive underground labyrinth that is Clearwell Caves, ancient iron mines in the heart of the Forest of Dean. The caves have been mined for over 2,500 years and all those centuries of tunnelling into the caves have now created more than 600 acres of caverns connected by miles of passageways, but don't worry, the marked way around the caves doesn't take you anywhere like that far.

Soon after we got into the caves themselves we came to the top of the narrow gauge railway that runs steeply away from the surface down into the depths of the mines and which was used to bring the rock to the surface. A distinct advance on the way it was once retrieved –

"Throughout the caves you can almost feel the presence of the men who worked down here"

children as young as six carried heavy loads in 'Billies' strapped to their backs – there's one report of a load of 60-70lbs being carried by a young boy! Indeed, the railway is still in use now, for ochre (used in paints) is extracted nowadays and can even be bought from the shop. So keep your eyes peeled and you may see the seams of oranges, reds, yellows and, I'm told, purples of this rich natural pigment whilst you are down there, and may be inspired to do a spot of decorating on your return home!

The caves are 100ft deep and you can walk through nine caverns underground which are laid out with equipment and displays of the old mining era. Throughout the caves, because time and the weather have little effect on them (only the constantly flowing water leaves its mark), you can almost feel the presence of the men who worked down here. "There's a cup, look," exclaimed my son "whose is it?" as we arrived at the miners' 'coe' where they went for their break and where you'd swear they'd just left and gone back to their picks and fire-setting.

When we emerged from the caves through the double doors into the shop, dragging a by-now empty buggy backwards (the only way to do it as the climb back to the surface is steep and fairly uneven), we decided to treat ourselves in the tearoom, where a fire blazed a welcome. We ate home-made cakes and our son was fascinated by all the mining memorabilia, especially the miners' lamps, suspended from the ceiling.

At Christmas, Clearwell is visited by Santa, and the caves are transformed into a series of stunning scenes in a Christmas fantasy, but be warned, it gets amazingly busy at weekends and it's better to visit on a weekday or make a very early start!

Puzzle Wood, just five minutes from Clearwell,

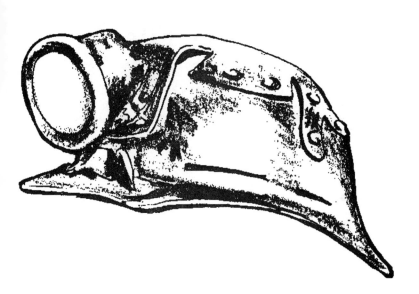

☞ sounded too intriguing to miss, so we drove into the car park and bought our tickets . . . with absolutely no idea of what we were about to discover. We walked down the path, past the farmhouse, detouring to have a look at the pig with her litter all sleeping peacefully, and walked into the wood. An amazing scene met our eyes. For Puzzle Wood is the home of ancient open iron workings, going back as far as the Romans and probably beyond. The paths through the wood are laid out as a puzzle, nothing as formal as a maze, and it's said that there is a trick to finding your way out quickly, but the atmosphere is so extraordinary and the wood so full of magic, that you'll be happy to be lost for a while. Choose a bright summer's day and as the sunlight filters through the canopy of trees you'll feel that you're in an enchanted forest.

Fact File

● ADDRESS: Clearwell Caves and Puzzle Wood, both near Coleford, Gloucestershire
● TELEPHONE: Caves 01594 832535, Puzzle Wood 01594 833187
● DIRECTIONS: M4/M48 to Old Severn Bridge, follow signs for Forest of Dean. A466 to Bigsweir Bridge, follow signs to Coleford then brown tourist signs
● PUBLIC TRANSPORT: None
● DISTANCE: 35-40 miles
● TRAVEL TIME: 60 minutes
● OPENING: Caves daily March to October, 10.00am-5.00pm. Puzzle Wood daily except Mondays, Easter to end October 11.00am-5.00pm
● PRICES: Caves adults £3.00, children £2.00, under-5's free. Puzzle Wood adults £2.00, children £1.50
● RESTAURANT FACILITIES: Yes
● NAPPY CHANGING FACILITIES: Yes
● HIGH CHAIRS: Yes
● DOGS: No
● PUSHCHAIR-FRIENDLY: No
● NEARBY: The Forest of Dean for walks and cycling

Museum of Welsh Life

This is more like two great days out, or more, as there's so much to see. Once you've been to St Fagans you'll want to go again and again. And one of its biggest pluses is that even at the height of the summer holidays when the car park is filled to capacity, this place is so big that it doesn't feel busy.

You walk through an impressive entrance foyer and out into the Museum itself. There are indoor galleries, but most of the interest is outside. We only had to mention the word "castle" for our four-year-old son to insist that we started our visit there, but when we reached it he was a little disappointed to discover that it had no battlements. The castle is, in fact, the original mansion house built on the site in 1580 and with its immaculate formal gardens and stepped fishponds gives a good idea of how the wealthy of Wales lived. Have a look round inside where it is furnished as a Welsh mansion of the early 19th century would have been. Don't miss the exquisite walled knot

"Atmospheric stories from Welsh legend are told in great dramatic style"

garden as you leave, or if you fancy a picnic, the top terrace above the gardens and fishponds where you'll find a bench underneath a vast tree which spread its branches generously and shadily above us as we ate our lunch.

All the buildings here, with the exception of the Castle, have been moved from their original locations around Wales to become part of the museum – the Derwen Bakehouse, for example, was built in 1900 in Aberystwyth. The buildings are scattered around the site to give the feeling of a wonderfully ramshackle village: with a surprise to be discovered everywhere you turn.

Head for the general store or bakehouse when you need some sustenance. Inside the bakehouse, bread is still baked to original recipes and sold in the tiny shop close by, while the general store offers other local produce and is set up just as you'd imagine an old-fashioned grocery shop. We particularly liked the ironmongery store alongside, with all its bits and pieces, but best of all was the photo studio, where you can dress up in any number of costumes and have your family portrait taken!

Armed with a cheesey bread roll we were sidetracked again, this time by storytelling in Nant-Wallter Cottage where, as our eyes slowly became accustomed to the darkness of the cottage, atmospheric stories from Welsh legend were told in great dramatic style.

Storytelling, that great Welsh craft, is done in both Welsh and English, during school holidays and is a great diversion.

There is so much to see at St Fagans that there's not room to mention it all, but the Rhyd-y-Car Iron Workers' houses (built around 1800 in

Merthyr Tydfil) can't be missed out. Each of the six houses in the small terrace has been decorated and furnished as it would have been at different periods since they were first built. So as you visit each in turn, you move from 1805 to 1855, 1895, 1925, 1955 and 1985, with each house providing a fascinating snapshot of life then.

Then there's the circular pigsty, a real hit with small children who can squeeze inside it (no pigs in residence!), the cockpit, the post office, the board school, the toll house and more. Plus the pottery, saddlery and smithy where you'll find at least one of the museum's working craftsmen in action at any time. The fact is that St Fagans will richly repay the time taken to get there.

Fact File

- ● ADDRESS: Museum of Welsh Life, St Fagans, Cardiff
- ● TELEPHONE: 01222 573500
- ● DIRECTIONS: M4 junction 33, A4232 and follow brown signs
- ● PUBLIC TRANSPORT: No.32 bus from Cardiff Central Station
- ● DISTANCE: 50 miles
- ● TRAVEL TIME: 90 minutes
- ● OPENING: All year, daily. 1 July to 30 September 10.00am-6.00pm; to 5.00pm the rest of the year
- ● PRICES: Adults £5.50, children £3.00, family £13.50, under-5's free. Reduced prices October to March
- ● RESTAURANT FACILITIES: Yes
- ● NAPPY-CHANGING FACILITIES: Yes
- ● HIGH CHAIRS: Yes
- ● DOGS: Yes (not in buildings)
- ● PUSHCHAIR-FRIENDLY: Yes
- ● NEARBY: Castell Coch (01222 810101), Caerphilly Castle (01222 883143)

Peat Moors
Iron Age
Visitor Centre

THE PERFECT PLACE TO SET YOUR CHILDREN'S IMAGINATIONS
alight: a trip back in time to spend a day in the Iron
Age. Wellies are a must for this visit so make sure
yours are all firmly on before you leap into history.

When the centre first opened in 1982 it consisted
of just one wooden building: a museum outlining the
history of the area and its traditional peat industry
and displaying some of the objects and artefacts that
had been unearthed locally. This museum is now just
the starting point of a visit to the
centre and offers a first
fascinating glimpse into
life in the Iron Age. The

amazingly well-preserved log boat particularly caught my children's attention, though I'm not sure they understood when I explained that they've discovered evidence of people living and working in the Somerset Levels and Moors as long ago as 4000 BC – last week is ancient history to them.

But it's when you leave the museum that you take a giant step back in time because here you'll find the most fascinating part of your visit – a reconstruction of an Iron Age settlement. We took a moment to look around and soak in the atmosphere as curly-horned Soay sheep wandered about in the mud among clusters of children who'd escaped the chores (actually a class of schoolchildren in authentic period dress on a visit to the centre, but they looked as if they belonged to the time and the place). Beyond lay the buildings around which settlement life revolved: the large and small roundhouses, the daub pits and pottery, as well as a turf-digger's shed and reconstructions of prehistoric trackways.

> ## "Making daub was fun, in a messy sort of way"

We couldn't wait to take a closer look, and headed first for the large round house where we discovered that prehistoric doesn't mean crude and flimsy. We tipped our heads backwards and marvelled at the intricately constructed and very solid thatched roof, and ran our hands over the wattle and daub walls to feel how firm these were too. Then we sat in the comfort of sheepskin-covered seats, feeling quite at home, to watch the fire being lit in the central hearth and to learn about how they cooked their food.

The best thing about the centre is the wealth and variety of activities on offer. Throughout the season there are all sorts of demonstrations and events geared to families. It's a good idea to

☞ check the programme and choose a day with something that will appeal to you. When we went we discovered a group of children learning how to make fences by weaving sticks through poles and couldn't resist joining in, though I doubt I'll be making my own next time we need a new fence. Nor am I going to be trying my hand at making daub – but it was fun in a messy sort of way: mixing up the clay, dung and chopped straw to create our own prehistoric building material.

For a thoroughly enjoyable history lesson that feels nothing like learning at all, this place is a must. We felt we'd had a real taste of another time and got a really good idea of what life must have been like. But home . . . and all those modern conveniences . . . was calling!

Fact File

- ADDRESS: Peat Moors Iron Age Visitor Centre, Shapwick Road, Westhay, near Glastonbury, Somerset
- TELEPHONE: 01458 860697
- DIRECTIONS: Between Shapwick and Westhay off the A39
- PUBLIC TRANSPORT: No
- DISTANCE: 55 miles
- TRAVEL TIME: 1 hour 30 minutes
- OPENING: Daily Easter to end October 10.00am-4.30pm, weekends only during March. Group bookings all year round
- PRICES: Adults £2.25, children £1.50, family £7.00
- RESTAURANT FACILITIES: In adjacent Garden Centre
- NAPPY CHANGING FACILITIES: No
- HIGH CHAIRS: No
- DOGS: No
- PUSHCHAIR-FRIENDLY: Yes, but it can get very muddy
- NEARBY: Shapwick Heath National Nature Reserve

Shambles Museum

WALKING DOWN CHURCH STREET, THE MAIN STREET IN NEWENT, there is little to alert you to the fascinating world that lies behind the entrance to the Shambles Museum. As you walk from the streets of the late 20th century through the doors into the museum itself, you find yourself magically transported back in time over 100 years to the world of the Victorians. For here, shoe-horned in behind Church Street is a re-creation of cobbled streets, alleys, shops workshops and homes all depicting aspects of Victorian life.

Buy a copy of the beautifully illustrated guide (50p) to ensure that you don't miss anything – with so many delightful hidden corners it's a distinct possibility. There's no doubt you'll enjoy the museum even if you don't have one, but you'll get many times the pleasure if you do. With so much to look at and wonder at, this is one of those lovely places that appeals to adults and children alike. My small son can't resist windows full of fascinating objects and there are plenty of shop windows here: the pawnbroker, the jeweller, the music shop and the post office with its

"What fascinated our four-year-old most were the tradesmen's workshops"

selection of typically Victorian greetings cards, the toyshop and the grocer. Everything we saw generated yet more questions, "what's that?", "what's that for?" and lots of "look!"s. But what fascinated our four-year-old most were the tradesmen's workshops – old bicycles, huge iron keys, hammers and gigantic wheels, old wagons, barrels and the carpenter's collection of tools. "Look at those huge swords!"– I looked. They were, in fact, saws. I doubt he had a double life as a duellist.

We wandered slowly through the cottage garden and pressed our noses against the window of the tin chapel. Though tempted, we decided not to stop for a cup of tea

at the teashop, but went on, keen to see everything and especially interested in the taxidermist who, on the evidence, would stuff anything regardless of size – pheasant chicks would you believe?

You can weave in and out of alleyways and climb stairs to see the beautiful conservatory above the doctor's dispensary (currently being restored to become a photographer's studio). Then, just when you think you've seen it all, you'll find yourselves at Fourstorey House, home to the draper and his family and looking as if they've just gone out for the day. Here we particularly liked the nursery with its collection of toys and furniture from another age – for our son it was clearly fascinating to see things, like high chairs and cots, dolls and other toys, that were at once familiar and utterly unfamiliar. Having climbed to the top of the house to see the maids' room we then went right to the bottom to have a look at

the washing cellar where you can see a prototype of today's washing machines. Then it was out through the well-stocked and very tempting gift shop and in the blink of an eye we'd landed back in the 1990's.

Fact File

- ● ADDRESS Shambles Museum, Church Street, Newent, Gloucestershire
- ● TELEPHONE: 01531 822144
- ● DIRECTIONS: M5 to junction 11, follow signs for Newent, then brown tourist signs
- ● PUBLIC TRANSPORT: No
- ● DISTANCE: 40 miles
- ● TRAVEL TIME: 60 minutes
- ● OPENING: 16 March to end December, Tuesday to Sunday and Bank Holidays, 10.00am-5.00pm or dusk if earlier
- ● PRICES: Adult £3.45, child £1.95, family £10.00
- ● RESTAURANT FACILITIES: Yes
- ● NAPPY-CHANGING FACILITIES: No
- ● HIGH CHAIRS: No
- ● DOGS: Yes
- ● PUSHCHAIR-FRIENDLY: Yes, but some stairs
- ● NEARBY: Three Choirs Vineyard (01531 890223) or Newent Lake

Somerset Rural Life Museum

"Goosey, goosey gander, whither do you wander?"

THIS WONDERFUL MUSEUM PROVIDES A GREAT OPPORTUNITY FOR children to discover how things were for Granny and Grandpa when they were young. It's all about Somerset farming activities and pastimes in the Victorian age, vividly brought to life throughout the year by a full series of workshops and demonstrations, many designed specifically to appeal to children. So it is well worth phoning in advance to find out what is on.

It's probably best to leave the buggy in the car and take babies or toddlers in a sling or backpack because the museum is on three floors of a large Victorian farmhouse with no lifts. Once inside, we went straight up the short flight of stairs from the entrance hall into the cowsheds. My three-year-old loved the exhibition of farming history housed in here, especially the stuffed horse harnessed to an old plough.

"Every aspect of traditional rural life explored"

There's lots more as well, with every aspect of traditional rural life explored: farming the land, bringing in the harvest, the ways in which produce was stored, cider making (including a recording of an old cider-maker singing an original wassail song), peat-cutting, basket-making and dairying. One not to miss is the exhibit that allows you to have a go at tiling a roof in the traditional way – it's quite a puzzle working out which way up the old pantiles go and how to place them so they overlap properly.

Emerge from the cowsheds into the old farmyard, where the atmosphere of the late 19th century has been re-created. Hens, ducks and geese scratch, waddle and wander around the wagons and waterpumps. One of our children backed away from the advances of an over-friendly gander and promptly sat in the water trough behind him. Fortunately, helpful staff managed to dry out trousers and pants before we left. Edging around the building so as not to attract the gander's attention again, we went into the beautiful 14th-century barn, where the roof is quite

stunning, a truly magnificent example of medieval workmanship, with the massive oak, chestnut and elm timbers supporting 80 tons of stone tiles! Down below on the ground, a muddle of wagons, tools, machines and wheels are on view, almost too many to see any of them very clearly! Back in the farmhouse we found a group of schoolchildren in the Victorian kitchen learning about the duties of a housemaid, so we made our excuses and climbed the stairs to look at the cradle-to-grave exhibition of a typical farm labourer. This is such a clever way to present history, with the focus on one individual really bringing the past to life. From a christening gown and cradle, through old school desks, clothes and a beer mug to a coffin wagon, you gain a real sense of the journey from birth through childhood, marriage and old age to death.

By the time we'd finished in the museum and visited the fantastic gift shop filled with far too many desirable items, the children were ready for some more physical activity. The museum caters well for school-aged children but younger ones may need to let off steam afterwards, so after a picnic in the Chalice Well gardens (where natural spring water bubbles to the surface) opposite the museum we headed for the swing park on the road into Glastonbury where there's loads of space for ball games and general running around. If we'd had any energy left we could have rounded our day off with a climb to the top of Glastonbury Tor, but we decided to leave that for another day.

Fact File

- ADDRESS: Somerset Rural Life Museum, Abbey Farm, Chilkwell Street, Glastonbury
- TELEPHONE: 01458 831197
- DIRECTIONS: M5 to junction 23, A39 to Glastonbury or A37/A39 via Wells
- PUBLIC TRANSPORT: Buses to Glastonbury and short walk
- DISTANCE: 40 miles
- TRAVEL TIME: 50 minutes
- OPENING: 1 April to 31 October Tuesday-Friday and Bank Holiday Mondays, 10.00am-5.00pm. Weekends 2.00pm-6.00pm. Tuesday-Saturday 10.00am-3.00pm from November to March
- PRICES: Adults £2.20, children 50p, family £5.00, under-5's free
- RESTAURANT FACILITIES: Yes
- NAPPY CHANGING FACILITIES: Yes
- HIGH CHAIRS: No
- DOGS: No
- PUSHCHAIR-FRIENDLY: No
- NEARBY: Glastonbury Abbey and Glastonbury Tor

Tintern Abbey & Tintern Old Station

"Bare ruin'd choirs where late the sweet birds sang"

JUST A HOP AND A SKIP OVER THE OLD SEVERN BRIDGE YOU'LL FIND the village of Tintern strung like beads alongside the River Wye and the undoubted jewel in the string is Tintern Abbey. There is something about ruined buildings that sends children's imaginations into overdrive and while we walked through the abbey grounds and into the spectacular church, now open to the sky and carpeted with close-cropped grass, our four-year-old and his friend were crawling through drainage gulleys and racing around on the grass, though not climbing on the walls (that's prohibited!). Places like Tintern make magical days out because everyone, big and little, gets something different out of them. For adults there is the historical interest; this was a Cistercian

> **"There is something about ruined buildings that sends children's imaginations into overdrive"**

abbey that was not only a place of work and of worship for the monks, but home as well – a self-contained community. Feel the unique atmosphere – even on a busy day the church feels tranquil and untouched by the twentieth century. For children it's the chance to scamper and romp in a different and unexpected kind of playground; one that is full of interesting nooks and crannies.

We left the Abbey and took the A466 north towards Monmouth and just five minutes up the road came to Tintern Old Station – the best reminder of the now defunct Chepstow to Monmouth railway line. It's extraordinary that little else remains of what would have been a fabulous journey through the past. However, the station is now home to a charming tea room which offers an extensive lunch menu or home-made cakes, the signal box houses a craft shop and a train forever on the sidings gives you a glimpse of how it used to be. And a shop provides a good selection of merchandise as well as comprehensive local information.

Tintern Old Station is one of our favourite trips. The playground, whilst not huge or novel, keeps children occupied for hours and if you head off in

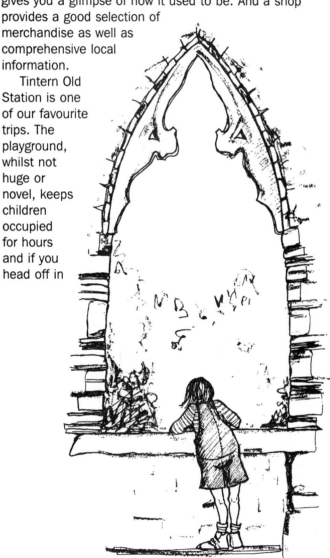

the opposite direction you can walk beside the miniature railway line down to the turntable and see where the bridge across the river used to be. Alternatively, climb down the steps to the riverbank and walk along through fields of sheep (pack wellies, we forgot ours last time and got very muddy!) to Brockweir and back for a well-earned cup of tea. Throughout the summer on certain days (though do ring and check first) the small steam train runs and children (and adults) love the ride to the turntable and back. The last time we went on a train day my son kindly saved us money by running beside the train instead of riding on it! If you have time on the way back down to Chepstow, take a detour at Lower Wyndcliff to marvel at the views – seven counties and the Severn Bridge are visible on a clear day.

Tintern village itself will repay a slow amble along its main street; among the interesting shops are a well stocked second-hand bookshop, antique shops and Tintern Pottery. Abbey Mill Centre too has craft shops and a cafe. Too often a day out fails to deliver because there's not quite enough to do. Tintern gives you a problem that's quite the reverse – plenty to do and too little time to do it in.

Fact File

- ADDRESS: Tintern Abbey and The Old Station, Tintern, Monmouthshire
- TELEPHONE: 01291 689251 (Abbey), 01291 689566 (Old Station)
- DIRECTIONS: M4/M48 over Old Severn Bridge and follow brown tourist signs
- PUBLIC TRANSPORT: Stagecoach Red & White buses from Chepstow or Monmouth (01633 266336)
- DISTANCE: 20 miles
- TRAVEL TIME: 40 minutes
- OPENING: Abbey daily 9.30am-6.30pm (to 4.00pm in winter). Station 10.30am-5.00pm 1 April to 1 November
- PRICES: Abbey adults £2.40, children £1.90, family £6.70, under-5's free. Station 50p parking
- RESTAURANT FACILITIES: Yes
- NAPPY-CHANGING FACILITIES: No
- HIGH CHAIRS: No
- DOGS: No abbey but yes station
- PUSHCHAIR-FRIENDLY: Yes
- NEARBY: Chepstow Museum (01291 625981)

Up, Down, There & Back

Avon Valley Railway

"Down at the station, early in the morning, see the little puffer trains all in a row"

YOU'LL FIND THIS CHARMING STEAM RAILWAY ON THE EDGE OF THE Cotswolds in the pretty village of Bitton. There are steam rides most Sundays from May to the end of September, and special event days, such as Thomas the Tank Engine or Teddy Bears' Picnic throughout the season. Static viewing is available the rest of the year, when the shop and buffet are open and you can see people working on the engines.

Calling on a special event day, we found ourselves transported into real Thomas the Tank engine land as we drove into the vast car park about a mile from the station and joined the queue to board a real old 'Bertie the Bus' to take us down the road to meet the friends of Thomas. Diesel, Grumpy and Peter the Pannier Tank were on the rails ready to take loads of excited children for a short (half an hour) trip up and down the length of line that has been restored. Plans are in hand to extend the track further towards Bath which will be great, because if there's one drawback to the Avon Valley Railway, it is that the train rides are too short and the view from the windows isn't all that thrilling,

"We had to have a chat with the Fat Controller, spats well cleaned and yellow waistcoat neatly buttoned"

but none of that matters much to train-mad kids! The first thing we had to do was have a chat with the Fat Controller who was patrolling the platform in true Fat Controller style, spats well cleaned and yellow waistcoat proudly adorning his girth. Once our son had had a (somewhat one-sided) chat with him about Henry being bricked into the tunnel (a favourite story from the video), we climbed on board Diesel and found ourselves seats in a compartment, sliding doors and all, with another family, whose father had clearly read every Thomas story written! As it was a corridor train there was only one window seat, but democracy ruled and our new friends had it on the outward journey and we all shuffled about on the way back. There was huge excitement from all of them every time we went under a bridge and clouds of steam billowed around the train. Children are always coming up with something to surprise their parents, but the knowledgeable, and entirely serious, way in which two three-year-olds discussed how the engine had to be uncoupled for the train to be turned round made it hard to keep a straight

☞ face. Who says videos aren't educational?

It is a short journey, but in some ways that's an advantage for the "when will we be there?" brigade, and if you visit, as it's best to, on one of the special days, there's lots more to do, with stalls and plenty of entertainment for the kids. Most kids, ours included, were really taken with a steeply inclining track down which they came, at a fair speed, in a little wooden truck – all operated manually, no machinery in sight. A bouncy castle had plenty of customers too, as did the miniature steam railway, though it was a mystery how the engine driver coped as he had steam blowing straight in his face whichever way the train was going!

Of course, the underlying purpose of these days is to raise money to maintain the railway and ensure that Thomas still has a line to run on, and among the fund-raising events was a balloon race, so we filled in a ticket with our name and address, watched our balloon being filled with helium and then gazed at the sky as it was lifted way up and out of our view. We're still waiting to hear how far it got, but our son thinks a cow has eaten it.

Fact File

● ADDRESS: Avon Valley Railway, Bitton Railway Station, Willsbridge Road, Bristol
● TELEPHONE: 0117 932 5538 or 0117 932 7296 (24-hour talking timetable)
● DIRECTIONS: A431 from Bristol
● PUBLIC TRANSPORT: Train from Bristol to Keynsham and 30-minute walk, or 332 bus from Bath or Bristol to Bitton
● DISTANCE: 5 miles
● TRAVEL TIME: 15 minutes
● OPENING: Steam rides every Sunday from May to beginning October, daily over Easter weekend. Static viewing all year every weekend 11.00am-5.00pm
● PRICES: Adults £3.00, children £2.00, family £9.50, under-3's free. Free for static viewing
● RESTAURANT FACILITIES: Yes
● NAPPY CHANGING FACILITIES: Yes
● HIGH CHAIRS: No
● DOGS: Yes
● PUSHCHAIR-FRIENDLY: Yes
● NEARBY: Avon Valley Country Park

The Gloucestershire & Warwickshire Railway

AHH, YOU CAN'T BEAT THE WHIFF OF COAL, STEAM AND ENGINE OIL IN the nostrils! Both big and small lovers of steam trains will get a nose-full of nostalgia here, as well as plenty to look at and steam rides through glorious Cotswold countryside. Originally part of the Great Western Railway, six and a half miles of track have been re-laid and restored since the Railway's demise in the late 1970's. Running from Toddington to Gotherington it is a round trip of 13 miles, taking about an hour station to station.

We started off at Toddington on a busy Vintage Steam Gala weekend, with many other people and cats-and-dogs worth of rain. Despite the crowds and the weather we managed to leap into an empty compartment almost immediately, pulled by the suitably impressively sighing and groaning Dumbleton Hall steam engine (big, black, circa 1929 beast to non-train spotters). With a blast of the whistle and a wave of the flag we were off, past the signal box, loco warehouses and

"With a blast of the whistle and a wave of the flag we were off"

finally the fields and trees of the open countryside. There are pretty villages to see on the way, bridges to cross, remains of a 13th century Cistercian Abbey ("like a dragon's castle"), and for the really observant, remnants of a medieval farming system ("a bit like a giant's lilo").

At Winchcombe you can get out to visit the signal box and see the renovation sheds full of carriages and wagons in various states of repair, before the train takes a deep breath and hauls itself up to the mouth of the tunnel. Wheee! it's a long one, and was the highlight of the day for our crew. It's on then to Gotherington where you can't get out but can watch from your carriage as the

engine is switched round to the other end of the train for the return journey.

Back at Toddington there was plenty to see and do on our visit, with steam fire engines, steam rollers, traction engines, motorcycles and fairground organs in full voice. All was bustle and noise and dripping steam. We particularly enjoyed the model display which ranged from steam engines to dolls' houses and from fairground rides to narrow boats. On non-Gala days there are still the signal box, running shed – a sort of garage for steam locomotives – and the engine repair workshops (although access is limited). On occasional summer Sundays there is a narrow gauge railway which offers 15-minute round trips.

The station cafe, the Flag and Whistle, has reasonably priced snacks and cakes, or there are picnic areas at both Toddington and Winchcombe. Winchcombe itself is a pretty town, about a mile's walk from the station. Lots of special events are planned for 1999 : Mother's Day, Easter Egg Hunts, Thomas the Tank, Teddy Bears Picnic, Steam Gala and good old Santa Specials around Christmas to name some. Ring to check days and times in advance.

Fact File

- ADDRESS: The Gloucestershire & Warwickshire Railway, Toddington Station, near Cheltenham, Gloucestershire
- TELEPHONE: 01242 621405
- DIRECTIONS: M5 junction 9, A46 towards Evesham then B4077 towards Stow. Go through Toddington and follow signs to railway
- PUBLIC TRANSPORT: Coach services by Castleways (01242 602949)
- DISTANCE: 55 miles
- TRAVEL TIME: 1 hour 30 minutes
- OPENING: 11.00am-5.30pm weekends and Bank Holidays from 14 March to end October. Diesel only weekends in February and November
- PRICES: Round trip adults £7.00, children £4.50, family £19.00, under-5's free
- NAPPY CHANGING FACILITIES: No
- HIGH CHAIRS: No
- RESTAURANT FACILITIES: Yes
- DOGS: Yes
- PUSHCHAIR-FRIENDLY: Yes
- NEARBY: Sudeley Castle (01242 603197)

West Somerset Railway

*"When you're the right side
of the footplate travelling
by steam"*

THE GREAT THING ABOUT THIS TRAIN JOURNEY IS THAT AS LONG AS
you start in the south you end up at the seaside, and for
all the small children I know there seems to be a
particular magic about this. In fact, there is something
about travelling by steam train that appeals to children of
all ages, including the very grown-up ones. Here you can
travel 20 miles from Bishops Lydeard to Minehead, with
10 restored stations along the route that you can
get off at.

Allow lots of time before your train leaves Bishops
Lydeard to explore and soak up the atmosphere of this
authentic period station.

"The children watched with delight as animals ran from the train as we passed"

We had a look at the
fireman shovelling coal
and stoking the
magnificent blaze to a
red hot roar, and then
whilst standing with
Grandpa on the road
bridge over the line, we
watched the smoke and steam as it billowed up from
under us and all around us. Perhaps not the healthiest of
activities but worth it to see the excitement on the
children's enthralled faces – so much better than the
fleeting thrill of an inter-city 125 flashing by. Back on the
platform we still had time for a quick look at the model
railway and a fleeting visit to the shop which stocked a
host of Thomas the Tank Engine and Friends products and
lots of other railway merchandise, before strolling along
beside the train to choose a good seat. Going for a table
seat in an open carriage the children pressed their faces

up against the window to wait for the train's departure. Then all at once, the doors banged shut, the station master and the guard exchanged a few words, the whistle blew and we were off.

At a leisurely pace the train heads north, winding through the Somerset countryside with the impressive Quantock hills to the east and beautiful mixed farm and woodland to the west. On reaching the beach at Doniford the line runs parallel to the coast for the rest of the journey to Minehead. It's a treat not having to concentrate on driving and being able to point out not just the interesting things, but the ordinary ones as well – people in their gardens, farmers working in their fields, cars on the roads and at the level-crossings. The children watched with delight as animals ran from the train as we passed, sometimes with a whistle and a great puff of steam. At Williton Station, a regular passing place for West Somerset Railway trains the children enthusiastically noticed another train full of families just like us passing close by. With noses up to the window pulling faces at the other children, they waved

☞ and dissolved into giggles. Then just as my eldest asked "Are we nearly there?", Granny suddenly said "Who can see the castle?" and the children immediately turned to the opposite window, all thoughts of sand and sandcastles temporarily forgotten, to see the real and fabulously impressive Dunster Castle perched high on the hill. Long before the new excitement of the castle wore off we pulled into the station at Minehead to a day of ice-creams, sand and water play, a picnic on the beach and lots of sand in our sandwiches.

If you don't fancy a day on the beach, there is still plenty to fill a day here. Try stopping off at one or more of the stations on the route for a country walk (Crowcombe Heathfield or Stogumber), picnic (Stogumber) or stroll along the beach (Blue Anchor). At Washford there is a small railway museum and a pub near the station, whilst at Dunster you can get off and take a 20-minute walk to the historic village itself. With special event days such as Thomas the Tank and Vintage Steam days on offer too it would be a shame to miss it!

Fact File

- ● ADDRESS: West Somerset Railway, The Station, Minehead, Somerset
- ● TELEPHONE: 01643 704996 or 01643 707650 (24 hour talking timetable)
- ● DIRECTIONS: M5 to junction 25 or 26 to Taunton, follow brown WSR signs to Bishops Lydeard. Bishops Lydeard is 4 miles from Taunton on the A358 to Minehead
- ● PUBLIC TRANSPORT: Number 28a bus from Taunton, or some special WSR buses (telephone 01823 272033)
- ● DISTANCE: 60 miles
- ● TRAVEL TIME: 1 hour 30 minutes
- ● OPENING: Sundays in March, most days April, May and October and daily in June, July and August
- ● PRICES: Return trip between Bishops Lydeard and Minehead £8.90 adults, £4.45 children or £24.00 family. Under-5's free
- ● RESTAURANT FACILITIES: At stations and buffet trolley on some services
- ● NAPPY CHANGING FACILITIES: Yes
- ● HIGH CHAIRS: No
- ● DOGS: Yes
- ● PUSHCHAIR-FRIENDLY: Yes
- ● NEARBY: Minehead, Dunster village and castle

The Sun Has Got His Hat On

Avebury Stone Circle

"Ring-a-ring-o'roses, a pocket full o'posies"

SUNRISE OVER THE REMAINS OF THIS MYSTICAL STONE CIRCLE MUST be quite something, but we got to the picturesque village of Avebury at noon with the sun already high in the sky. If you park in the centre of the village you'll find yourselves already inside the great henge. In fact, most of the village buildings, including the pub, post office and chapel, some of them with stolen stones in their walls, are all neatly contained inside the huge circle of Avebury. The pretty church with its surrounding thatched wall and the Elizabethan manor house are just outside it on the western edge.

"We used the children as markers in a game called 'where the stones once stood'"

We set off to discover and enjoy the space (and exercise) the circle provides. The first stone we came to was the Barber stone, so-called after it fell over and killed an itinerant barber-surgeon in the 14th century. Don't worry, it's been set upright securely now. The massive ditch surrounding the stones would once have been an impressive 30 feet deep, but today, much less deep, its grassy slopes provide a superb natural play space, perfect for running, jumping, rolling and tumbling. From the road heading south we looked along West Kennet avenue. This was originally a processional avenue a mile and a half long lined on either side by 200 paired stones, alternately elongated and diamond shaped.

The roads running through Avebury cut the circle neatly into quarters so cross the road to explore the next sector. Here the children found a marvellous chair-like stone that they loved climbing up to sit in. We also found the stump of the ring stone and the remains of the southern inner circle within which the mighty Obelisk once stood.

With our backpacks and baskets we must have looked as if we were on a month's trek, but it was only a short walk along the ridge of the outer bank and well worthwhile as, here to the east, the circle is fringed by beautiful beech trees and we found the perfect spot for our picnic. Pack bats and balls, blankets and books as well as lots of food and drink if you come here as you'll probably want to stay a while. Grown-ups and children alike can have such a good time; exploring tree roots; roly-poly racing into the ditch; sliding and somersaulting over the grass banks. Revived by our picnic and the children calmed down a little with a

couple of stories on the blanket we eventually packed up and went on round the circle, where we found ourselves in a stretch where few stones remain. Here we had fun using the children as markers in a game called 'imagine where the stones once stood'!

Head back into the village for ice-creams (the kids) and a browse in the shops (grown-ups). There are two museums in the grounds of Avebury Manor: the Wiltshire Folk Life Museum in a wonderful old barn, and the archaeology museum in a converted stable which has finds from the local area. Older children and adults can immerse themselves here for at least an hour: alternatively 'Stones' restaurant has some fabulous cakes!

With fantastic walks, nature-made playgrounds and fascinating history, there really is something at Avebury for everyone, ensuring we all had the best day out. And the children learned a thing or two, namely that 'mega' means big and 'lith' means stone – but that's enough archaeology for one day!

Fact File

- ADDRESS: Avebury, Wiltshire
- TELEPHONE: 01672 513989 (Marlborough tourist information)
- DIRECTIONS: M4 to junction 16, A4361 south from Wroughton or A4 Bristol, Bath, Chippenham, Calne, Avebury
- PUBLIC TRANSPORT: Thamesdown bus 49A Swindon/Devizes. Wilts & Dorset 5/6 Salisbury/Swindon (0345 090899)
- DISTANCE: 30 miles
- TRAVEL TIME: 45 minutes
- OPENING: All year
- PRICES: Free
- RESTAURANT FACILITIES: Yes
- NAPPY CHANGING FACILITIES: Yes
- HIGH CHAIRS: Yes
- DOGS: Yes
- PUSHCHAIR-FRIENDLY: Yes
- NEARBY: West Kennet Long Barrow, Silbury Hill, Ridgeway walk, Windmill Hill

Avon Valley Country Park

WHAT A FIND! WE FOLLOWED THE SIGNS TO AVON VALLEY COUNTRY Park with some disbelief as the road took us through a fairly run-down industrial estate then drove into the park and on to the vast grass car park with grins on our faces. From the minute we parked the car we knew this was one of those perfect places and that we were going to have a good time. Don't forget to pack your nets if you fancy a bit of pond-dipping, and bring your own coal if you want to use one of the barbecues provided in the picnic area.

We arrived closer to lunchtime than elevenses so our first move was to have our picnic – car park is too urban and formal a description of the setting we were in, parked as we were away from other cars at the top of a green field that rolled gently down towards the river.

Not surprisingly, the adventure playground beat pets' corner into first place for a visit and it's a really good one with something for kids of all ages, though I want mine to reach 18 before they think of flinging themselves off the top of the drop slide – which does just that – drops vertically for several feet before curving to give the slider the slide of her life.

"We strolled along mown paths through the fields beside the river"

Once we'd prised our son off the wooden train we set off on the riverside trail, which is where Avon Valley Country Park scores really highly for families. All the way along the trail we found signpoints which related to the free brochure we were given as we arrived. This brochure is packed with information: it doesn't just tell you what you'll see but offers interesting snippets such as the problems presented by wild mink (they made it very difficult to persuade the ducks to settle on the lake), how to prevent frost nipping the fruit trees in the bud and the fact that there have been wallabies living wild in England since 1850. In the first field we came to there was a boating lake with (free) rowing boats – "Can I have a go, pleeease?" "Yes, Daddy, course you can" said our son, so the baby and I took a slow amble around the lake while Daddy rowed up, down and round.

Boat trip over, we strolled on along mown paths through the fields beside the river (keep an eye on young children). There is lots to see and do along the way. Apart from the animals, including rare breeds of cattle, Shetland ponies and golden Guernsey goats, each of the fields along the walk contains a single piece of play equipment, part of a one and a quarter mile children's

☞ assault course – a small feature, but one that provides more evidence of how much thought has been given to making Avon Valley Country Park a thoroughly enjoyable experience for everyone.

A little further on we came upon a small drama, namely a goat who'd managed to get her head through a wire fence but now, because of her horns, was well and truly stuck. "Let's go and tell the man," our son insisted and dragged us almost at breakneck speed through the rest of what we'd intended to be a relaxed meander past the deer park and the wallaby pen. We found that we weren't first with the news and someone had already set off to rescue the goat. Not for the first time, as it seems to be her new party trick!

Fact File

- ADDRESS: Avon Valley Country Park, Pixash Lane, Bath Road, Keynsham, Bristol, Avon
- TELEPHONE: 0117 986 4929
- DIRECTIONS: A4 from Bristol towards Bath and follow signs
- PUBLIC TRANSPORT: Bus X39 from Bristol or Bath to Keynsham
- DISTANCE: 5 miles
- TRAVEL TIME: 20-30 minutes
- OPENING: March 27 to October 31, 10.00am-6.00pm, closed Mondays except Bank Holidays and during school holidays
- PRICES: Adults £3.50, children £2.50, under-2's free
- RESTAURANT FACILITIES: Yes
- NAPPY CHANGING FACILITIES: Yes
- HIGH CHAIRS: No
- DOGS: No
- PUSHCHAIR-FRIENDLY: Yes
- NEARBY: The National Trust's Dyrham Park (0117 937 2501)

Broadway Tower Country Park

DON'T FORGET TO PACK YOUR SAUSAGES AND COME TO BROADWAY for the definitive 'Picnic with a View'. There's a choice of two walks through breathtaking countryside, a tower to climb, adventure playground, and plenty of space to run around, picnic or barbecue your own food.

As we approached Broadway (a very pretty village in its own right) we had a competition to see who could spot the Tower first. I forget who won, but it is not hard to identify, standing majestically right on the edge of the Cotswolds. A folly built in the 1700's in the midst of a picturesque and romantic landscape, it was later a holiday retreat to William Morris, and is now a country park area with plenty to offer those wanting to blow away cobwebs. It is quite exposed though, so on a windy day pack warm clothes.

Escaping from the car, the children made a beeline for the Tower. There is a stairs-up and stairs-down system to get to the top, which means it is all very orderly and no little feet get trodden on. With only 75 steps up our 5-year-old declared it 'easy-peasy climbing', but you'll want to keep hold of young ones when you get to the top, as it is a dizzy experience with a vast view.

"Several picnic areas with tables and superb views"

It wasn't clear enough to see the Welsh mountains on the day we visited, but apparently you can on some days, and 12 counties too.

On the way down, look in on the exhibitions of the history of the tower and William Morris, and then back outdoors again, where you'll have to decide whether to do the walk before or after your picnic and playtime.

There is choice of two walks: a straight 45-minute stroll along the ridge and back, or a longer, one hour 30 minutes' circular ramble through rolling countryside over stiles, down the slope and up again. Both are clearly

marked
on maps you
are given on
arrival, and both
also form part of the Cotswold Way. Should you be feeling
really energetic you could always suggest that you do the
100-odd miles on to Bath!

The longer walk can be a mite muddy in places and
strenuous for those with a pushchair – you'll have to lug
it over a few stiles too. However, it makes a pleasant
walk, not too long for small legs, and there is always the
adventure play area to bribe them with afterwards.

Back near the entrance are the animal enclosures,
home to a herd of very tame red deer, and rare breeds of
Highland cattle and Cotswold sheep. Next on is the
adventure area, carefully sited out of the wind in the
shelter of trees. It proved fun and exciting, with all the
usual equipment including aerial runway and trampoline.
The suggested route was a test of stamina and strength
over timber and rope, certainly not for softies but ideal for
budding Gladiators.

There are several picnic areas set aside with picnic

tables and superb views. For the intrepid, barbecues are provided, both under cover or in the open, and charcoal is on sale at the shop. If you've had enough of burnt sausages, the Rookery Barn serves good hot and cold snacks, and has a delightful terrace where you can linger whilst supervising a giant game of draughts or chess on an enormous chequered board.

Fact File

- ● ADDRESS: Broadway Tower Country Park, Broadway, Worcestershire
- ● TELEPHONE: 01386 852390
- ● DIRECTIONS: M5 junction 9, A46 to Evesham, then the A44 towards Stowe and Oxford. Signposted six miles south-east of Evesham
- ● PUBLIC TRANSPORT: Buses from Broadway, Evesham and Chipping Campden
- ● DISTANCE: 50 miles
- ● TRAVEL TIME: 1 hour 30 minutes
- ● OPENING: Daily Easter to 31 October, 10.00am-6.00pm. Tower only weekends October-March (weather permitting)
- ● PRICES: Adults £3.00, children £2.20, under-4's free. Family £9.00
- ● NAPPY CHANGING FACILITIES: Yes
- ● HIGH CHAIRS: Yes
- ● RESTAURANT FACILITIES: Yes
- ● DOGS: Yes, except in Tower
- ● PUSHCHAIR-FRIENDLY: Yes, except in Tower
- ● NEARBY: Broadway Teddy Bear Museum (01386 858323)

Charmouth Beach

"One, two, three, four, five, once I caught a fish alive"

JANE AUSTEN FOUND CHARMOUTH AN AGREEABLE PLACE FOR 'SITTING in unwearied contemplation' and the same can still be said of the town today. Charmouth is set amongst the gentle rolling hills of West Dorset overlooking Lyme Bay and flanked by lovely walking country.

The beach itself is a wide bay with a mixture of pebbles, shingle and fine sand and a wide expanse of good firm sand exposed to the west of the river at low tide. This makes it the ideal spot for football, sandcastles and crab racing with lots of shallow rock pools left behind to explore. The tide was in when we arrived and, not liking the surprise of weed-covered rocks underneath me when I'm swimming, we opted to go into the water from the beach in front of the concrete steps. After a huge picnic lunch, still damp from the morning's swim but not allowed back in the water, the children dragged us across to the rock pools with hastily bought fishing nets to do some serious exploring now that the tide had gone out. They were

"You can join a guided fossil hunt most days"

captivated by the tiny crabs we found underneath the rocks and the tiny fish that had stayed behind and now darted swiftly around their pools. Travelling light is never an option when you've got children, but Charmouth is kind to heavily-laden beachgoers, with parking close to the beach and two cafe/beach shops from which to buy ice-creams, snacks, buckets and spades, cups of tea and more ice-cream.

To the east of the beach is a good, though strenuous cliff path rising 500 feet to Stonebarrow Hill which, if you haven't exhausted yourselves swimming as we did, you can climb up and down before going up again to the top of the 617 foot high Golden Cap. I've always assumed that it's called that because of the way that the honey-coloured rock glistens like gold in the sunshine, but perhaps I'm being whimsical! When I was a child my parents used to send us children racing up to the top of the Golden Cap, ensuring that they got a good rest by saying they'd stay at the bottom to count how long it took us. For now, we decided just to admire the landscape

☞ while the children had a final swim – far less tiring!

To the West of Charmouth you can wander in to the picturesque coastal town of Lyme Regis and enjoy an ice-cream whilst watching the fishing boats gently bobbing in the shelter of the cobb, the long outcrop of rock, made famous forever when Meryl Streep stood dramatically at the end in *The French Lieutenant's Woman*. Either side of Charmouth beach, the cliffs are black, muddy clay and as a result fairly unstable, but full of fossils. Children and adults flock to these cliffs hoping to make a big discovery like the one 12-year-old Mary Anning made in 1811 when she found a fossilised Ichtyosaurus that's now in London's Natural History Museum. You can join a guided fossil hunt most days from the heritage centre at Charmouth beach – ring first to check times of fossil-hunting walks.

And if you happen to be in the area on Christmas Day, and you're feeling brave, you could astound friends and family by joining in the annual Christmas charity dip. You'll certainly deserve your brandy-soaked Christmas Pudding after that!

Fact File

- ADDRESS: Charmouth Beach, Charmouth, Dorset
- TELEPHONE: 01297 560772 (Heritage Centre on beach)
- DIRECTIONS: A35 Bridport to Axminster road, follow signs to the beach
- PUBLIC TRANSPORT: None
- DISTANCE: 80 miles
- TRAVEL TIME: 1 hour 30 minutes
- OPENING: All year
- PRICES: Free (charge for car park)
- RESTAURANT FACILITIES: Yes
- NAPPY CHANGING FACILITIES: Yes
- HIGH CHAIRS: No
- DOGS: No
- PUSHCHAIR-FRIENDLY: At low tide once you're over the pebbles
- NEARBY: Lyme Regis town and cobb

Forest of Dean Sculpture Trail

"If you go down to the woods today, you're sure of a big surprise"

THE FOREST OF DEAN IS FULL OF HIDDEN TREASURES AND Beechenhurst Lodge is a real gem – a lovely open spot in the heart of the forest and the starting point for the Sculpture Trail, an intriguing open-air exhibition of sculptures, all celebrating, commemorating and reflecting the life of the forest and the people who live and work in it.

We discovered, too late unfortunately, that this is not a walk to be undertaken without a map. Your first stop has to be at the cafe at the Lodge to buy your map (50p), otherwise, like us, you'll finally find your way back to the start having had a quite wonderful if confusing ramble, and only then

"The giant chair towered above us as we stood underneath the seat"

spot the sign that marks the start of the trail on which it states very clearly "Don't set off without a map". But this is another day out that will triumph over any slight setback. Funnily enough, we had seen the sign because we followed it to set off – we were just too keen to read it properly!

As you climb up the track between the trees the first, and biggest, of the sculptures comes into view – a giant chair made from whole tree trunks that just got bigger and bigger the closer we got to it, towering above us as we stood underneath the seat. The Sculpture Trail is one of those great places where nature, with a bit of a helping hand in this case, creates a perfect playground, as we discovered when we came upon Black Dome, a circle of 900 pieces of charred larch rising to a dome in the centre, created to become part of the forest again as natural decay takes its course. The children thought this was wonderful to climb all over and would have stayed all day, but we wanted to see what else we could find and the next thing turned out to be a sculpture called Iron Road by Keir Smith, a run of 20 carved sleepers set on a disused railway line, each one depicting an aspect of forest life and its industrial past – a stunning thing to come across and the children were fascinated as they tried to make out what was carved on each one. Following one of the blue arrows that tell you you've arrived at another exhibit we turned off the main path and found ourselves in the Grove of Silence where, high up on the trees, plaques bearing the word silence in different languages draw your attention to the peace of the forest. Along another part of the trail the children were captivated by the giant acorn and scots pine cone carved in stone and lying on the ground as if they had just fallen from their parent trees. We also happened on a stream beside which lay several iron canoes apparently slowly decaying. As these didn't appear on the map, when we got hold of one, we're still not sure whether they formed part of the trail or were a happy accident.

By the time we made it back to the Lodge it was late in the afternoon but still gloriously warm and we were thrilled to discover that we could still get a cup of tea at quarter to six on a September afternoon! And the biggest bonus of all was that we could drink it in peace while children who'd been too tired to walk 10 minutes earlier rallied miraculously at the sight of the swings and slide!

Fact File

- ADDRESS: Sculpture Trail, Beechenhurst Lodge, Cinderford, Gloucestershire
- TELEPHONE: 01594 827357 or 01594 833057 (Forest Enterprises)
- DIRECTIONS: M4/M48 over old Severn Bridge, A48 to Lydney, then follow brown tourist signs to Beechenhurst Lodge
- PUBLIC TRANSPORT: No
- DISTANCE: 50 miles
- TRAVEL TIME: 60 minutes
- OPENING: Sculpture trail, daily all year; Lodge daily 10.00am-6.00pm from March to October, 10.00am-4.00pm weekends only in winter
- PRICES: Car park £1.50
- RESTAURANT FACILITIES: Yes
- NAPPY CHANGING FACILITIES: Yes
- HIGHCHAIRS: No
- DOGS: Yes
- PUSHCHAIR-FRIENDLY: No
- NEARBY: Clearwell Caves and Puzzle Wood

Other Books IN THE SERIES

Orders

ALL OTHER BOOKS IN THE SERIES ARE AVAILABLE FROM:
The Heinz Guide to DAYS OUT WITH KIDS
BON•BON VENTURES
24 ENDLESHAM ROAD
LONDON SW12 8JU
TEL: 0181 488 3011
FAX: 0181 265 1700

AND OUR WEB SITE **www.daysoutwithkids.co.uk**
PAYMENT MAY BE MADE BY CREDIT CARD (ACCESS/VISA/MASTERCARD), OR BY
CHEQUE /POSTAL ORDER PAYABLE TO BONBON VENTURES. PLEASE ALLOW
£1.00 POSTAGE AND PACKING FOR THE FIRST BOOK, AND 50P PER BOOK
FOR SUBSEQUENT BOOKS.

- ✂

ORDER FORM

PLEASE SEND ME A COPY/IES OF HEINZ GUIDE TO DAYS OUT WITH KIDS
(TICK REQUIRED)

☐ *MIDLANDS EDITION*
    PRICE £4.99 & £1.00 POSTAGE AND PACKING

☐ *NORTH WEST EDITION*
    PRICE £4.99 & £1.00 POSTAGE AND PACKING

☐ *NORTH EAST EDITION*
    PRICE £4.99 & £1.00 POSTAGE AND PACKING

☐ *WEST COUNTRY EDITION*
    PRICE £4.99 & £1.00 POSTAGE AND PACKING

☐ *SOUTH EAST EDITION*
    PRICE £5.99 & £1.00 POSTAGE AND PACKING

I ENCLOSE MY
REMITTANCE OF
£ _____

NAME _____

ADDRESS _____

_____

_____

_____

I WISH TO PAY BY CREDIT CARD
CARD NUMBER ☐ ☐ ☐ ☐ ☐ ☐ ☐ ☐ ☐ ☐ ☐ ☐ ☐ ☐ ☐ ☐

EXPIRY DATE   / _____

SIGNED _____

Notes

Notes

Notes

Notes

Strange But True...

Fascinating facts about the nation's favourite family brand

 Only four people in the whole world know the secret blend of spices used in Heinz Baked Beans

 Each day Heinz uses enough tomatoes to fill an Olympic size swimming pool

 Every year Heinz uses 26,000 tonnes of vegetables, fruits and cereals, 60 million eggs, four million gallons of milk and 7,000 tons of meat

 Enough cans of Heinz baby food are made to feed every British baby a can a week

 Seven hundred cans of soup are made every minute

 Camelford in Cornwall has its own Heinz Cream of Tomato Soup Appreciation Society. To join the club, you must take a blindfolded taste test and pick out Heinz tomato soup from the other brands